Field Guide to

North American Flycatchers

Field Guide to

North American Flycatchers

Empidonax and Pewees

Cin-Ty Lee
Illustrated by Andrew Birch

Princeton University Press
Princeton and Oxford

Copyright © 2023 by Princeton University Press

Princeton University Press is committed to the protection of copyright and the intellectual property our authors entrust to us. Copyright promotes the progress and integrity of knowledge. Thank you for supporting free speech and the global exchange of ideas by purchasing an authorized edition of this book. If you wish to reproduce or distribute any part of it in any form, please obtain permission.

Requests for permission to reproduce material from this work should be sent to permissions@press.princeton.edu

Published by Princeton University Press
41 William Street, Princeton, New Jersey 08540
99 Banbury Road, Oxford OX2 6JX

press.princeton.edu

All Rights Reserved

Names: Lee, Cin-Ty, author. | Birch, A. (Andy), illustrator.
Title: Field guide to North American flycatchers : empidonax and pewees / Cin-Ty Lee ; illustrated by Andrew Birch.
Description: First edition. | Princeton, New Jersey : Princeton University Press, [2023] | Includes bibliographical references and index.
Identifiers: LCCN 2022030138 (print) | LCCN 2022030139 (ebook) | ISBN 9780691240626 (pbk.) | ISBN 9780691244327 (e-book)
Subjects: LCSH: Flycatchers--North America--Identification. | Bird watching. | BISAC: NATURE / Birdwatching Guides | NATURE / Reference
Classification: LCC QL696.P2 L545 2023 (print) | LCC QL696.P2 (ebook) | DDC 598.8/23--dc23/eng/20220729
LC record available at https://lccn.loc.gov/2022030138
LC ebook record available at https://lccn.loc.gov/2022030139

British Library Cataloging-in-Publication Data is available

Editorial: Robert Kirk and Megan Mendonça
Production Editorial: Mark Bellis
Cover Design: Wanda España
Production: Steve Sears
Publicity: Matthew Taylor and Caitlyn Robson
Copyeditor: Frances Cooper
Typesetting and design: D & N Publishing, Wiltshire, UK

Cover illustrations by Andrew Birch
Page ii: Olive-sided Flycatcher (top); Gray Flycatcher (bottom).
Page iii: Alder Flycatcher (left); Acadian Flycatcher (right)

This book has been composed in Minion Pro (body) and Ariana Pro (headings)

Printed on acid-free paper. ∞

Printed in China

10 9 8 7 6 5 4 3 2 1

CONTENTS

Field Guide to

North American Flycatchers

Preface

This book is the product of a lifelong dream to tackle the identification of some of the most challenging groups in field identification. The two of us met at Berkeley in the early 1990s when we were college students. Together, we worked on a variety of short identification articles focused on advanced topics for various birding magazines. The most satisfying topics were identification challenges that required a more holistic approach: not just focusing on plumage features but also looking at overall structure, shape, size, and impression.

It is always exciting trying to present this information in an easily accessible format to as wide an audience as possible. For some birds, such as shorebirds, sparrows, and flycatchers, there are a dizzying number of field marks to remember for each bird, surely a barrier to entry except for the most experienced birders. How can one bring all these features together into what skilled birders call "gestalt" or overall impression, and more importantly, show that this holistic approach is in fact better, especially when out in the field? Equally importantly, how does one communicate general impressions in a way that everyone understands?

We have been interested in the *Empidonax* flycatchers and pewees for as long as we can remember. *Empidonax* flycatchers are often thought to be impossible to identify, and it certainly seemed that way 50 years ago, but each decade brought new advances from the birding community. A decade ago, we decided that we wanted to take what we knew then as a community and make *Empidonax* identification a possibility for everyone. This book is the product of our obsession with chasing and studying flycatchers across the country. In this book, you will learn how to see subtle structural differences, calibrate your ears to the subtleties of their calls and songs, and incorporate migration timing into your toolkit. We do not guarantee that you will be able to identify every single flycatcher. We ourselves cannot identify all of them and we are not embarrassed to admit that we can still make mistakes. However, we hope the approach here will take you a few steps closer and together we will learn as a community.

No book is written in a vacuum. So many people have influenced us. We continue to be inspired by the works of Kenn Kaufman. His *Field Guide to Advanced Birding* was pioneering in introducing gestalt birding to the community. His *Field Guide to Birds of North America* is an example of simplifying bird identification for the masses. And, of course, we devoured his early *Birding* articles on the field identification of *Empidonax*. We were also inspired by the illustrations of David Sibley, Lars Jonsson, and many others, whose greatest contributions, among many, were to convey gestalt through their illustrations. Similarly, the beautifully illustrated Japanese field guides by Osao Ujihara and Michiaki Ujihara were truly inspirational. There are so many other exceptionally talented artists that it seems offensive to only name a few, but the works of Jen Brumfield, Peter Burke, James Coe, Catherine Hamilton, Hans Larsson, Ian Lewington, Brian J. Small, Darren Woodhead, and Julie Zickefoose were often referenced for inspiration when creating the illustrations. The importance of migration timing was instilled in us early by the likes of Jon Dunn, Kimball Garrett, and Paul Lehman. Alvaro Jaramillo's works set the bar for not overlooking any detail.

We are also indebted to the entire eBird team at the Cornell Laboratory of Ornithology as well as the thousands of amateur birders that contribute data to eBird so that the timing and movements of birds are now known better than ever before. We are indebted to the countless birders who contributed audio recordings to xeno-canto and Cornell's Macaulay Library of bird sounds and photographs. Arch McCallum's detailed analyses of *Empidonax* vocalizations helped us better understand and portray calls and songs.

Our journey of several decades with flycatchers benefited from the expertise of many: Eugene and Steve Cardiff, Ted Eubanks, the late Ned K. Johnson, Douglas Morton, Raymond Paynter, and Ron Weeks. We thank Ned K. Johnson and Carla Cicero for access to study specimens at Berkeley and Gary Voelker for specimens at Texas A&M. Terry Chesser and Carla Cicero provided insight on phylogeny. Wenrong Cao introduced us to the world of QGIS. Our work benefited from many eyes, including those of Alvaro Jaramillo, Oscar Johnson, Tom Stephenson, and Ron Weeks. Any mistakes, of course, are our own.

In 2020, the impacts of the COVID-19 pandemic provided the impetus for us to finish the project as it seemed then that any one of us could drop dead the next day. We could not have done this without the support of our respective families (Yu-Ye, Heru, Tiffany, Chloe, and Henry), which has allowed us to pursue our obsessions.

CIN-TY LEE, Rice University, TX
ANDREW BIRCH, Los Angeles, CA
JULY 2022

INTRODUCTION

To the novice birder, flycatchers all seem to look alike. Even among
experts, there is often disagreement on the identity of the same
bird. The challenge of flycatcher identification is that no single field
mark is diagnostic. The field marks of flycatchers are subtle, based
mostly on differences in color contrast, shape, and relative lengths
of tail and wings. Many of these features are variable with overlap
between species. These subtleties and the intrinsic variabilities of
field marks are further complicated by observer bias. For example,
one person's long tail may be another person's medium-length tail; or
the perception of color, a feature we often take for granted, may be
influenced by lighting conditions (such as shading or leaf reflections)

or the observer's own eye. An *Empidonax* flying in and out of shade can appear to change color!

In this guide, we try to demystify flycatcher identification and make it more accessible. Although a single field mark is rarely useful in identifying flycatchers, the combination of multiple field marks, including vocalizations, is unique for a given species. These combined field marks result in unique overall impression or gestalt. This guide will help you learn this holistic approach in field identification. In the first part of the guide, you will learn how to calibrate your eye to these subtle field marks, honing your skills in seeing relative differences in shape, size, length, and color contrasts rather than absolute quantities. You will also learn how to separate species by their calls. In the second part of the guide, we apply these concepts to the identification of each species. We also show how knowledge of range, habitat, and migratory schedules can aid in identification.

Of course, not all flycatchers will be identifiable, but we hope this guide will help you see and hear all birds in a new way and make you a better birder.

What Are Empidonax and Pewees?

The *Empidonax* flycatchers and *Contopus* pewees are a subset of the family *Tyrannidae*, also known as the tyrant flycatchers, one of the largest bird families in the world. The tyrant flycatchers are predominantly insectivores with most displaying the distinctive behavior of flycatching. Flycatchers will typically sit on a prominent perch from which they can see insects fly by and repeatedly sally out to catch insects on the wing. The family consists of 101 genera with a total of 425 species, all restricted to the Americas. Although they share a common name with the flycatchers in Europe, Asia, and Africa, the Old World flycatchers are in an unrelated family, *Muscicapidae*.

This book covers all members of the *Empidonax* and *Contopus* genera (pewees and wood-pewees) recorded in the United States. We have also included one member of the genus *Mitrephanes* (Tufted Flycatcher) because of its superficial resemblance to some of the *Empidonax* flycatchers. Members of *Empidonax* and *Contopus* exhibit striking similarities in appearance, but genetic differences, combined with differences in song, nesting behavior, habitat preference, distribution, and migratory pattern indicate that they are distinct species with ancient divergence.

Phylogenetically, the *Empidonax* flycatchers can be grouped into four distinct clades based on the studies of Johnson and Cicero (2002), Fjeldså et al. (2018), and Harvey et al. (2020). One group includes Pine, Dusky, Gray, Hammond's, Least, and Buff-breasted Flycatchers, which tend to be dull in color and nest in open shrublands or woodlands. The second includes the greenish/yellowish flycatchers: Pacific-slope, Cordilleran and Yellow-bellied, which prefer shaded understory habitats. The third includes the Traill's Flycatcher complex of Alder and Willow, which nest in dense thickets near streams. The fourth consists only of the Acadian Flycatcher, which is the most phylogenetically unique *Empidonax*. The order in which we describe each species in this guide is based on the most recent phylogeny of Harvey et al. (2020).

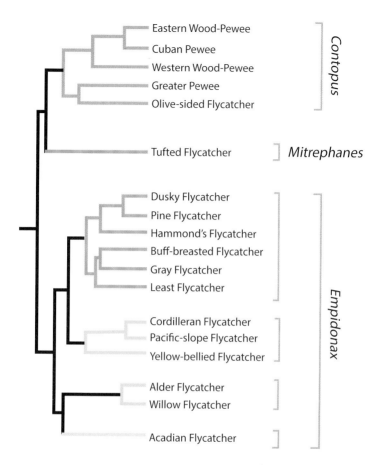

Eastern Wood-Pewee
Cuban Pewee
Western Wood-Pewee
Greater Pewee
Olive-sided Flycatcher

Contopus

Tufted Flycatcher

Mitrephanes

Dusky Flycatcher
Pine Flycatcher
Hammond's Flycatcher
Buff-breasted Flycatcher
Gray Flycatcher
Least Flycatcher

Cordilleran Flycatcher
Pacific-slope Flycatcher
Yellow-bellied Flycatcher

Alder Flycatcher
Willow Flycatcher

Acadian Flycatcher

Empidonax

How to Use
This Guide

HOLISTIC FIELD IDENTIFICATION

The challenge of flycatcher and pewee identification is that individual field marks are subtle, variable, and often overlap between species. Identification thus depends on not one field mark but a combination of field marks. Focus on shape, proportions, and contrasts rather than absolute size, length, and color, which are difficult to judge in the field without direct comparisons to other flycatchers or because of variable lighting conditions and observer bias.

Use our illustrated field mark diagrams on the following pages to calibrate your eyes and ears to these subtle field marks. While all field marks are important, some are more valuable in field identification and these are discussed first, followed by those field marks that are more subtle. Always remember that there will be some birds that will defy identification.

TOPOLOGY OF A FLYCATCHER

The illustration (p.10) summarizes the main parts of a flycatcher one should study. On the head, note the crown shape, forehead angle, shape and boldness of the eye-ring, paleness of lores, size of the bill, and color of the lower mandible. Features such as the eyeline, supercilium, auriculars and malar are often distinctive in other bird species, but are less so in *Empidonax* and *Contopus*.

Color contrasts between upperparts (mantle and nape) and underparts (throat, chest, and belly) should be noted. On the wing, pay attention to the boldness of the upper and lower wingbars, any contrasts between the stacks of the secondary feathers (upper wing panel, including tertials) and primaries (lower wing panel), and the length of the primary projection relative to the secondaries. Tail length relative to the body and wings and other structural features should also be noted.

TOPOLOGY OF A FLYCATCHER

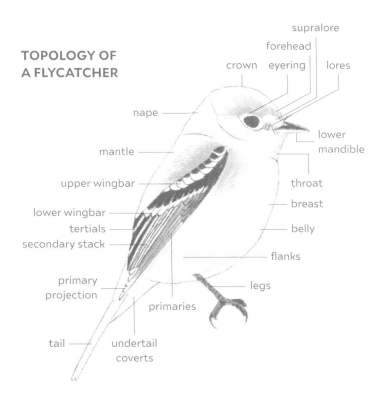

RELATIVE HEAD SIZE is categorized into large, medium, and small relative to the body. Hammond's Flycatcher appears proportionately large-headed; Least, medium-headed; and Dusky, small- to medium-headed.

CROWN SHAPE includes: crested, as in Pacific-slope and Cordilleran Flycatchers or pewees; peaked as in Acadian Flycatcher; rounded as in Least Flycatcher; and flat-topped as is often the case for Gray Flycatcher. Willow Flycatcher often has a more peaked crown than Alder Flycatcher.

CROWN SHAPE

ROUND

Alder
Willow
Yellow-bellied
Hammond's
Dusky
Least
Buff-breasted

FLATTISH

Dusky
Gray

PEAKED

Olive-sided
Greater Pewee
Wood-Pewees
Cuban Pewee
Acadian
Willow
Pacific-slope
Cordilleran
Hammond's
Dusky
Pine
Least

CRESTED

Tufted
Olive-sided
Greater Pewee
Wood-Pewees
Cuban Pewee
Pacific-slope
Cordilleran
Pine

FOREHEAD ANGLE corresponds to the angle of the forehead slope where it meets the base of the bill. A steep forehead angle corresponds to near vertical, as commonly seen in Hammond's Flycatcher; a shallow forehead angle describes most Acadian Flycatchers; and most other flycatchers have intermediate forehead angles.

FOREHEAD ANGLE

SHALLOW

Olive-sided
Greater Pewee
Wood-Pewees
Cuban Pewee
Acadian
Gray

INTERMEDIATE

Tufted
Olive-sided
Greater Pewee
Wood-Pewees
Cuban Pewee
Acadian
Alder
Willow
Yellow-bellied
Pacific-slope
Cordilleran
Dusky
Pine
Gray
Least
Buff-breasted

STEEP

Tufted
Hammond's
Pine
Buff-breasted

BILL LENGTH ranges from small to medium to long. Acadian Flycatchers have long bills whereas Hammond's and Least Flycatchers have small bills. Bill width can sometimes be a useful field mark although bill width is often difficult to evaluate unless seen from below. Least, for example, tends to have a wide-based bill, but there is overlap with other flycatchers.

BILL LENGTH

LONG

Olive-sided
Greater Pewee
Wood-Pewees
Cuban Pewee
Acadian
Gray

MEDIUM

Tufted
Olive-sided
Acadian
Alder
Willow
Yellow-bellied
Pacific-slope
Cordilleran
Dusky
Pine

SMALL

Tufted
Hammond's
Least
Buff-breasted

LOWER MANDIBLE COLOR is not always diagnostic because it can be variable within a given species. Nevertheless, it can be a useful supporting field mark when observed well. The main criterion is to determine whether the lower mandible is all dark, all orange/yellow, or partly orange/yellow. Most flycatchers have lower mandibles with pale bases and dark tips, but it can be useful to appreciate the full range of variation. For example, an all dark bill is typical of Hammond's Flycatcher; an all pale yellow or orange lower mandible is typical of Pacific-slope, Cordilleran, and Acadian Flycatchers.

LOWER MANDIBLE COLOR

MOSTLY OR ALL
ORANGE/YELLOW

Tufted
Olive-sided
Greater Pewee
Eastern Wood-Pewee
Cuban Pewee
Acadian
Alder
Willow
Yellow-bellied
Pacific-slope
Cordilleran
Pine
Gray
Least
Buff-breasted

PARTLY ORANGE/YELLOW

Willow
Alder
Dusky

DARK

Western Wood-Pewee
Hammond's
Dusky

RELATIVE TAIL LENGTH is evaluated by comparing tail length with the overall body size and projection of the primaries. Specifically, relative tail length refers to the exposed tail; that is, the length of the tail that projects beyond the tip of the primaries. Tail length is described as short, medium, or long; for example, Hammond's Flycatcher has a relatively short tail; Least, short to medium; Willow and Alder, medium; and Gray, long.

RELATIVE TAIL WIDTH is a measure of the width of the base of the tail (where the tail meets the body). Tail width can be evaluated by comparing it to body size. Acadian Flycatchers have the widest tails. Willow and Alder Flycatchers have medium tail widths. Most other flycatchers have narrow tails. Flycatchers with narrow tails often show a slight narrowing of the tail toward the body, whereas those with medium to wide tail widths tend not to show any narrowing. Note that tail width can be variable.

OUTER-TAIL FEATHER coloration can potentially be a useful field mark, but this should be used with care. If the outer-tail feathers are whitish, there is a good chance it is a Gray Flycatcher. However, the outer fringes of a tail, particularly when backlit by the sun or on a worn bird, can often look pale, giving the impression of white outer-tail feathers for any flycatcher.

TAIL LENGTH
MEASURED FROM TIP OF PRIMARIES

SHORT   MEDIUM   LONG

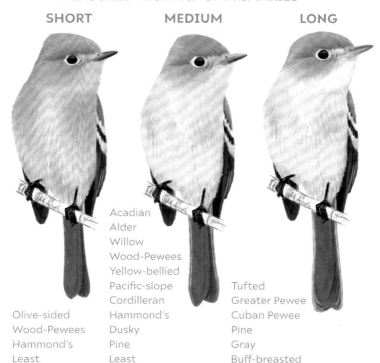

Acadian
Alder
Willow
Wood-Pewees
Yellow-bellied
Pacific-slope
Cordilleran
Hammond's
Dusky
Pine
Least

Olive-sided
Wood-Pewees
Hammond's
Least

Tufted
Greater Pewee
Cuban Pewee
Pine
Gray
Buff-breasted

TAIL WIDTH

NARROW

Tufted
Yellow-bellied
Pacific-slope
Cordilleran
Hammond's
Dusky
Pine
Gray
Least
Buff-breasted

WIDE

Olive-sided
Greater Pewee
Wood-Pewees
Cuban Pewee
Acadian
Alder (medium)
Willow (medium)

PRIMARY PROJECTION is a measure of how far the primaries project beyond the exposed tertials in the secondaries. It is evaluated by comparing the length of the projection with the length of the longest tertial on a *folded wing*. A primary projection that is more than two-thirds the length of the tertials is long (e.g., Acadian and Hammond's Flycatchers and especially pewees) and less than half is short (e.g., Least and Gray Flycatchers). Intermediate primary projections are seen in Willow and Alder Flycatchers. Yellow-bellied Flycatchers have intermediate to long primary projection. Note that the primary projection may vary slightly with age and sex, and also that molt or posture influences the perception of primary projection. When the bird's wings are held in a more spread-out manner, primary projection can appear long because one's eye is drawn to the base of the secondaries rather than the longest tertial.

Primary projection may appear longer on birds with their wings drooped and primaries and secondaries spread. Primary projection should always be assessed relative to the tip of the longest tertial.

PRIMARY PROJECTION
RELATIVE TO TERTIALS

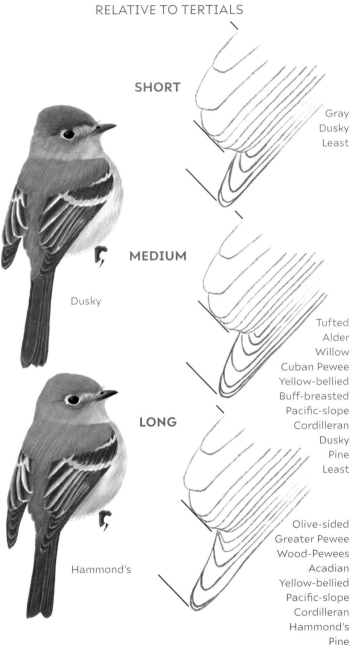

SHORT

Gray
Dusky
Least

Dusky

MEDIUM

Tufted
Alder
Willow
Cuban Pewee
Yellow-bellied
Buff-breasted
Pacific-slope
Cordilleran
Dusky
Pine
Least

LONG

Olive-sided
Greater Pewee
Wood-Pewees
Acadian
Yellow-bellied
Pacific-slope
Cordilleran
Hammond's
Pine

Hammond's

WINGBAR CONTRAST is the extent to which the pale wingbars stand out against the dark wings and upperparts (mantle). For example, the wingbars of Gray and Dusky Flycatchers show low to medium contrast because the wingbars are not as bright, and the wings are dark, but not black. In contrast, because of the black ground color of their wings, Least and Yellow-bellied Flycatchers both exhibit strong wingbar contrast, even though the color of their wingbars is different (Least = whitish, Yellow-bellied = slightly yellowish). Another useful way to assess wingbar contrast is to compare the lightness of the wingbar with that of the bird's mantle. In Least Flycatchers, the wingbars are significantly brighter than the mantle, whereas in Gray and Dusky Flycatchers, the wingbars are similar in brightness to the mantle. In Hammond's Flycatchers, the wingbars are only slightly brighter than the mantle, but not to the extent seen in Least.

UPPER AND LOWER WINGBAR RELATIVE CONTRAST can be a useful trait in evaluating pewees, but not so much in evaluating flycatchers. The upper wingbar on Western Wood-Pewees tends to be less bold than the lower wingbar, whereas the wingbars on Eastern Wood-Pewees tend to be of similar boldness.

WINGBAR CONTRAST
RELATIVE TO UPPERPARTS

WEAK

MEDIUM

Olive-sided
Greater Pewee
Wood-Pewees
Cuban Pewee
Willow
Dusky
Gray

Tufted
Eastern Wood-Pewee
Alder
Willow
Pacific-slope
Cordilleran
Hammond's
Dusky
Pine
Buff-breasted

STRONG

Acadian
Yellow-bellied
Least
Buff-breasted

WING PANEL CONTRAST is the overall contrast between the stacks of the secondaries (upper wing panel) and primaries (lower wing panel) on the folded wing. This is the overall impression of wing panel brightness imparted by how pale or bright the feather edgings are (specifically the anterior margins of the secondary and primary feathers). In all empids, the edges of the secondary feathers are brightly colored, often giving a crisply patterned secondary stack, which manifests as a pale upper wing panel when seen from a distance. However, the extent of pale edge on the primary feathers varies from species to species. In some, like Yellow-bellied and Least Flycatchers, the feather edges are dark or dull, making the lower wing panel appear solid black, which contrasts with the pale-edged secondary stack and results in a strong wing panel contrast. In Pacific-slope and Cordilleran Flycatchers, the primaries have extensive pale edges, resulting in weak contrast between upper and lower wing panels. For the grayer flycatchers, the order of increasing wing panel contrast is Gray, Dusky, Hammond's, and Least.

WING PANEL CONTRAST
SECONDARY PANEL vs PRIMARY PANEL

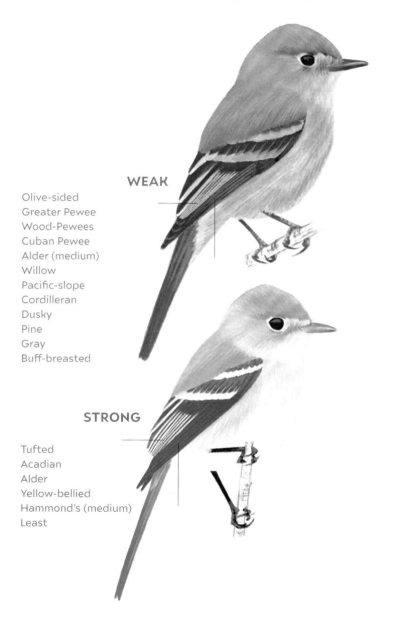

WEAK

Olive-sided
Greater Pewee
Wood-Pewees
Cuban Pewee
Alder (medium)
Willow
Pacific-slope
Cordilleran
Dusky
Pine
Gray
Buff-breasted

STRONG

Tufted
Acadian
Alder
Yellow-bellied
Hammond's (medium)
Least

UPPER/UNDERPART CONTRAST can be a useful supporting field mark. Instead of focusing on absolute color, which can be misleading, focus on the relative contrast between the upperparts (mantle, nape, and crown) and the underparts (throat, chest, and belly). The Least Flycatcher typically has a whitish throat and chest, which contrast strongly with its light brown mantle. In Hammond's Flycatcher, the chest tends to be slightly dusky with an intensity in color nearly identical to that of the mantle, resulting in weak upper/underpart contrast. This difference in upper/underpart contrast is particularly useful in separating Least and Hammond's Flycatchers, even under poor lighting conditions. Dusky and Gray both have weak upper/underpart contrast. Acadian shows strong upper/underpart contrast. Yellow-bellied, Pacific-slope, and Cordilleran Flycatchers, despite their bright overall colorations, have weak to medium upper/underpart contrast.

UPPER/UNDERPART CONTRAST

WEAK	MEDIUM	STRONG

Tufted	Eastern	Olive-sided
Greater	Wood-Pewee	Acadian
Pewee	Cuban Pewee	Alder
Wood-Pewees	Alder	Least
Cuban Pewee	Willow	
Yellow-bellied	Dusky	
Pacific-slope	Buff-breasted	
Cordilleran		
Hammond's		
Dusky		
Pine		
Gray		
Buff-breasted		

EYE-RING refers to the pale feathering surrounding the eye. Eye-ring types include teardrop-shaped, crisp, messy, and indistinct. Some flycatchers have limited to no eye-ring (indistinct), such as Alder and Willow Flycatchers and the pewees. Others, such as Pacific-slope, Cordilleran, Least, Hammond's, Gray, and Acadian Flycatchers, have complete eye-rings, but they vary in shape. In Pacific-slope and Cordilleran, the complete eye-ring is elongated at the rear of the eye, generating a diagnostic teardrop shape. In Yellow-bellied and Acadian, the eye-ring is complete with crisp borders. Least, Hammond's, Dusky and Gray often have complete eye-rings, but their borders may be more diffuse, giving a messier appearance. Eye-ring shape tends to be variable between individuals, resulting in considerable overlap, and, except for the extremes (teardrop-shaped and crisp complete eye-rings), eye-ring shape or boldness should not be used alone as a field mark.

LORES can be pale or concolorous with the crown. Pale lores are often touted as diagnostic for some flycatchers, like Dusky. However, many flycatchers can show pale lores, so this field mark is of limited use.

EYE-RING

TEARDROP

Cuban Pewee
Pacific-slope
Cordilleran
Pine

CRISP

Acadian
Yellow-bellied

MESSY

Hammond's
Dusky
Pine
Gray
Least
Buff-breasted

INDISTINCT

Tufted
Olive-sided
Greater Pewee
Wood-Pewees
Alder
Willow

OVERALL COLORATION can be categorized into gray, brown, olive, greenish-yellow, and orangish. Pacific-slope, Cordilleran and Yellow-bellied Flycatchers are examples of greenish-yellow, and Gray and Dusky Flycatchers are examples of gray or brown. Buff-breasted Flycatchers have orangish tones. Most other *Empidonax* species can display a continuous color spectrum between gray, brown, and olive. Some variability within a species is caused by wear and age. Summer birds tend to be the most worn and dull, whereas birds in juvenal or winter plumage (after finishing a complete molt) can appear more brightly and crisply colored. It is important to appreciate that color depends on lighting conditions and an observer's own perception. Except for the extremes, too much emphasis on color is not recommended. Instead, color contrasts between different parts of the bird should be the focus.

OVERALL COLORATION

GRAY

GREENISH-YELLOW

Cuban Pewee
Pine
Dusky
Pine
Gray

Acadian
Yellow-bellied
Pacific-slope
Cordilleran

Olive-sided
Greater Pewee
Wood-Pewees
Cuban Pewee
Alder
Willow
Hammond's
Dusky
Pine
Gray
Least

OLIVE/GRAY/BROWN

Behavior

WING FLICKING is practiced by many *Empidonax*. However, those with narrow tails, such as Hammond's, Least, Dusky, Yellow-bellied, and Pacific-slope/Cordilleran Flycatchers, tend to flick their wings often. Gray Flycatchers may occasionally flick their wings. Acadian, Willow, and Alder flick their wings less frequently. Pewees seldom flick their wings.

TAIL MOVEMENTS are helpful supporting field marks. Care must be taken to distinguish between tail pumping/flicking and tail dropping. In tail pumping/flicking, the tail is rapidly brought upward and then downward at the same speed. In tail dropping, the tail is rapidly brought upward, but dropped more slowly. The Gray Flycatcher is the only flycatcher to display tail dropping. Tail pumping/flicking is practiced by those with narrow tails, such as Hammond's, Least, Dusky, Yellow-bellied, and Pacific-slope/Cordilleran Flycatchers, with Dusky being the most frequent tail pumper in general. Acadian, Willow, and Alder, which have wider tails, pump or flick their tails less frequently. Pewees (except for Cuban) rarely pump/flick their tails.

Age and Molt

In many songbirds, winter and breeding plumages are strikingly different, but in flycatchers and pewees, there is no significant difference between winter and breeding plumages. Nevertheless, flycatchers and pewees regularly molt to replace worn feathers. Flycatchers and pewees undergo two molts a year: a prebasic molt (transitioning to winter plumage) and a limited prealternate molt (transitioning to breeding plumage). First-year birds undergo partial prebasic molts, but adults go through much more extensive prebasic molts during which most if not all flight feathers are replaced. Prealternate molts are limited, often involving only some covert, tail, and body feathers.

The timing of molt relative to migration differs between species and can sometimes be helpful in identification. The Wood-Pewees and Olive-sided Flycatcher complete their prebasic molts mostly on their wintering grounds, which means that during fall migration adults can appear quite worn while spring migrants appear fresh. Adult Yellow-bellied and Willow/Alder Flycatchers also complete most of their prebasic molts on the wintering grounds and thus appear worn in late summer. In contrast, adult Acadian and Hammond's Flycatchers molt on their summering grounds, so Acadian and Hammond's appear fresh during fall migration. Adult Least, Dusky, and Pacific-slope/Cordilleran Flycatchers may begin molt on the summering grounds (coverts) but complete their molts on the wintering grounds (flight feathers) and thus may appear to have a mixture of fresh covert feathers and worn flight feathers during fall migration.

Prebasic molts in first-year birds are typically less extensive than those of adults and often commence on the summering grounds. Juvenal plumages are usually very fresh looking. In some species, juvenal wingbars can have a buffy tint (e.g., Least, Acadian, and Yellow-bellied Flycatchers). Juvenal primaries tend to be slightly longer than adult primaries.

In summary, wingbars and the pale edges to secondary (including tertials) and primary feathers tend to be crisper and bolder after a molt. Worn birds appear duller overall, often with frayed feather edges, which reduces the boldness of wingbars and gives the impression of pale edges to the primaries and secondaries. Wear and tear can also give the impression of pale edges to tail feathers, so summer or early fall birds should be scrutinized.

Vocalizations

Flycatchers and pewees have distinct calls and songs. Their calls are often diagnostic, but many are only separated with considerable experience or careful analysis of spectrograms. We provide spectrograms here, but to convey the nature of the songs or calls in words, a few definitions are in order. Songs are described first by the number of syllables or notes, along with a mnemonic. The most important qualities of a song are: which note is accented, whether a particular note is rising or descending in frequency, and whether a note has a burry/buzzy or clean (whistle-like) quality. The note that is accented is expressed in capital letters, and the length of each mnemonic segment (e.g., number of letters) reflects the length of the note. In the spectrograms provided, which are frequency versus time diagrams, sound volume (amplitude) is represented by how bold the spectrogram is. A "*whit*" is represented by a rising spectrogram, with a soft "*whit*" showing a slight inflection and a sharp "*whit*" being steep. A "*pip*" is represented by a peaked spectrogram (i.e., inverted "V" shape). Slurs are represented by a downward inflection followed by a rise. Burry calls are represented by a broad frequency band.

Whenever possible, record vocalizations. One does not need sophisticated equipment. A smartphone's microphone suffices. Audio recordings can be visualized as spectrograms with a variety of free software, such as Audacity, or by simply uploading into eBird.org and xeno-canto.org databases.

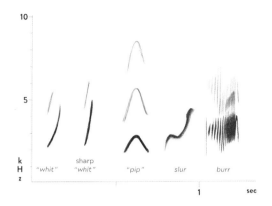

10

5

k
H
z

"whit"   sharp   *"pip"*   *slur*   *burr*
          "whit"

1   **sec**

Habitat Preference

Flycatchers have specific microhabitat preferences during breeding, but during migration they may still associate with microhabitats that resemble their breeding grounds. For example, even during migration, Olive-sided Flycatchers almost always sit on the tops of tall dead snags, Gray Flycatchers tend to be in more open brushy habitats. Yellow-bellied, Pacific-slope, Cordilleran, and Acadian Flycatchers tend to occur in more shaded habitats, and Willow and Alder tend to be in more open or woodland edge habitats. Some, like Hammond's and Dusky, do not have strong microhabitat preferences on migration or in winter. In any case, microhabitat preference should be used with caution during migration because migrants may have to make do with whatever is available at a stopover site.

(p.38)
During the breeding season, open, brushy habitat (*top*) suits Gray and often Dusky Flycatchers. Western, Yellow-bellied and Acadian prefer more shaded and often wetter habitats (*bottom*).

Range, Seasonal Status, and Migration

Always note the date, location, and habitat when observing a flycatcher or pewee. *Empidonax* flycatchers and pewees all migrate, summering in the north and wintering in Central America or South America. Arrival times, especially during spring, can differ substantially between species as they are synchronized with the life cycle of their primary food source—insects—which is strongly controlled by temperature. The more northerly the breeding range, the later the arrival. For example, in the east, Alder, Willow and Yellow-bellied Flycatchers do not arrive as spring migrants in the United States until May, while Acadian, which breeds in the southeastern United States, arrives in early April. Temperatures warm earlier in the spring along the Pacific coast than in the interior west (Rocky Mountains), so some western species like Gray, Dusky, Pacific-slope and Hammond's may already be on the move in mid-March in California, but arrival of their interior counterparts is delayed until April.

Most flycatchers and pewees are rare in the United States during winter because insects, which are their primary food source, are in short supply in winter. A few species, such as Gray, Hammond's, Dusky and Pacific-slope Flycatcher, winter in small numbers in southern California, southern Arizona, and Texas. In some winters Least can be fairly common along the Texas coast. In general, any wintering *Empidonax* in the United States should be studied carefully because many may turn out to be vagrants.

Range maps showing migration timing accompany each species account. On the range map, orange corresponds to the breeding range, blue the wintering range, and yellow the migratory range. Note that migration also takes place within the breeding and wintering ranges. On the range map, dotted contour lines show arrival times for fall and spring migrants at weekly intervals. Seasonal abundance charts show the full migration window at specific locations. Careful attention should be paid to weekly arrival contours as flycatchers tend to be faithful to arrival and departure dates from year to year. Fall birds may linger beyond the dates noted on the map.

We have also drawn arrows depicting approximate migration routes. Flycatchers of western North America typically follow the north–south aligning mountain ranges characteristic of the west. They may follow the foothills, canyons, or ridgelines. In most cases, arrival on northwestern breeding grounds, such as along the Pacific coast north to Alaska, is earlier than the same species' arrival in the mountains of the continental interior (Montana, Colorado, Utah) as the rise in temperatures in these interior mountains in spring lags those of the more humid Pacific coast.

Flycatchers and pewees of eastern North America predominantly follow a western circum–Gulf of Mexico route along the Texas coast in both spring and fall. Small numbers of some species take an eastern route, hopping along the Caribbean islands between Florida and Central America. Trans-Gulf migration between Louisiana and the Yucatan Peninsula is probably rare. Because most of the spring migration of eastern flycatchers is dominated by the western circum-Gulf route, most flycatchers are rare or uncommon in the spring in the southeast as most turn northward along the upper Texas coast. In the fall, migration often includes a more easterly component such that certain flycatcher species that were rare in spring in Louisiana, for example, become common as a fall migrant. A fraction of these southbound birds may head down through Florida and to Central America, although most continue along the western Gulf of Mexico. Much more work is needed to unravel the nuances of flycatcher migration.

TROUBLESOME FLYCATCHER

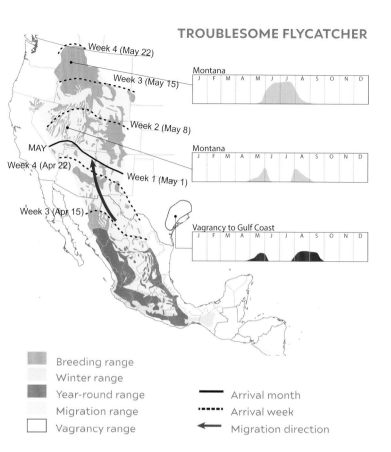

Week 4 (May 22)
Week 3 (May 15)
Week 2 (May 8)
MAY
Week 4 (Apr 22)
Week 1 (May 1)
Week 3 (Apr 15)

Montana
J F M A M J J A S O N D

Montana
J F M A M J J A S O N D

Vagrancy to Gulf Coast
J F M A M J J A S O N D

Breeding range
Winter range
Year-round range
Migration range
Vagrancy range

Arrival month
Arrival week
Migration direction

Summary

While no single field mark is in general diagnostic, the combination of field marks forms a unique "fingerprint" for a given species, even when considering the intrinsic variabilities of individual field marks. We have tabulated these features for each species in the following **FIELD MARK MATRIX** and comparison plate. Use these as a cheat sheet to help you remember some of the salient features of each species.

   We also provide a **VISUAL SIMILARITY MAP**, on which birds are arranged spatially according to how similar they appear. For example, Willow and Alder Flycatchers are nearly identical and thus displayed as overlapping fields. However, Alder Flycatcher shows some subtle similarities with Least Flycatcher, whereas Willow Flycatcher shows subtle similarities with wood-pewees. As another example, Gray, Dusky, Hammond's, and Least, in that order, form somewhat of a continuum. This visual similarity map was not derived from any phylogenetic considerations, but we note that some groups of visually similar species are indeed taxonomically related.

THE FIELD MARK MATRIX

		Tufted Flycatcher	Olive-sided Flycatcher	Greater Pewee	Western Wood-Pewee	Eastern Wood-Pewee	Cuban Pewee	Acadian Flycatcher	Alder Flycatcher	Willow Flycatcher	Yellow-bellied Flycatcher	Pacific-slope/Cordilleran Flycatcher	Hammond's Flycatcher	Dusky Flycatcher	Pine Flycatcher	Gray Flycatcher	Least Flycatcher	Buff-breasted Flycatcher	your bird
Crown shape	round																		
	peaked																		
	flat																		
	crested																		
Forehead angle	shallow																		
	medium																		
	steep																		
Bill length	short																		
	medium																		
	long																		
Lower mandible	all dark																		
	partial																		
	all orange/yellow																		
Tail length	short																		
	medium																		
	long																		
Tail width	wide																		
	medium																		
	narrow																		
Primary projection	short																		
	medium																		
	long																		
Wingbar contrast	strong																		
	medium																		
	weak																		
Wing panel contrast	strong																		
	medium																		
	weak																		
Eye-ring	indistinct																		
	messy, distinct																		
	bold, crisp																		
	tear-shaped																		
Upper/underpart contrast	strong																		
	medium																		
	weak																		
Wing flicking	often																		
	occasional																		
	rarely																		
Tail flicking	often																		
	occasional																		
	rarely																		
	tail dropping																		

HOLISTIC APPROACH
STRUCTURE, PLUMAGE, AND VOICE

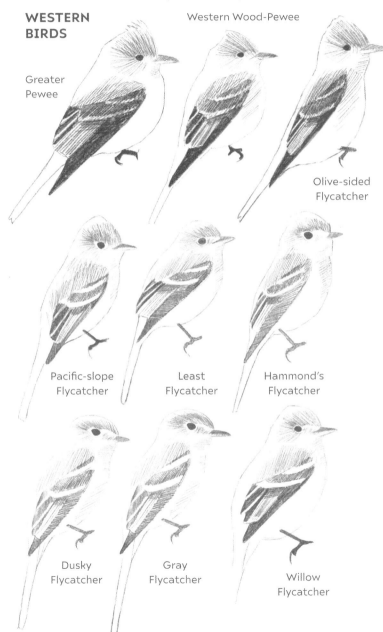

WESTERN BIRDS

Western Wood-Pewee

Greater Pewee

Olive-sided Flycatcher

Pacific-slope Flycatcher

Least Flycatcher

Hammond's Flycatcher

Dusky Flycatcher

Gray Flycatcher

Willow Flycatcher

HOLISTIC APPROACH
STRUCTURE, PLUMAGE, AND VOICE

EASTERN
BIRDS

Eastern
Wood-Pewee

Olive-sided
Flycatcher

Least
Flycatcher

Alder
Flycatcher

Willow
Flycatcher

Yellow-bellied
Flycatcher

Acadian
Flycatcher

VISUAL SIMILARITY MAP

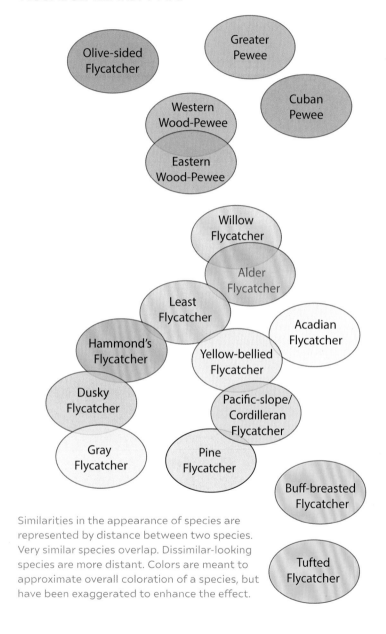

Similarities in the appearance of species are represented by distance between two species. Very similar species overlap. Dissimilar-looking species are more distant. Colors are meant to approximate overall coloration of a species, but have been exaggerated to enhance the effect.

46

The Field Guide

Tufted Flycatcher

Mitrephanes phaeocercus

L 4.7–5.3″ (12.0–13.5 cm), WT 0.3 oz (8.5 g)

GENERAL IDENTIFICATION The Tufted Flycatcher is unmistakable with its pointed crest and overall buff to cinnamon tones. Other distinguishing features are its small size, blackish wings, relatively bold white wingbars, lack of distinct eye-ring, small bill with entirely orange lower mandible, relatively long tail, and medium to long primary projection. The Tufted Flycatcher flicks its wings and tail but usually only just after landing. Its tail flicking is unique: a short but rapid succession like a fluttering or flickering, which makes the bird appear to shiver just after landing.

VOICE Tufted Flycatcher gives a variety of calls. It frequently gives a single note "*pip*" call. Tufted also gives a high pitched down-slurred whistle "*peeur*" similar to the "*peeur*" of Hammond's, but at a higher frequency. Its song consists of a rapid succession of "*pip*" notes or a distinctive "*chuwee-chuwee.*" Each "*chuwee*" phrase is characterized by an initial downward inflection in pitch followed by a drawn-out burry up slur.

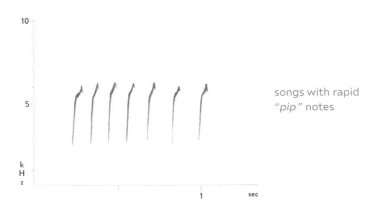

songs with rapid "*pip*" notes

TUFTED FLYCATCHER

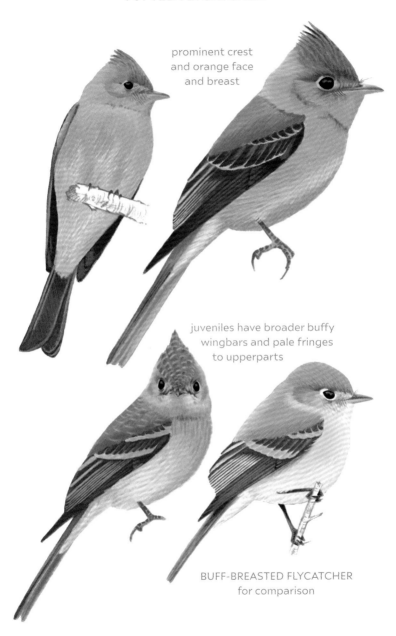

prominent crest
and orange face
and breast

juveniles have broader buffy
wingbars and pale fringes
to upperparts

BUFF-BREASTED FLYCATCHER
for comparison

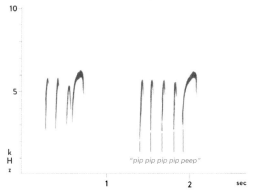

songs with rapid
"pip" notes

"pip pip pip pip peep"

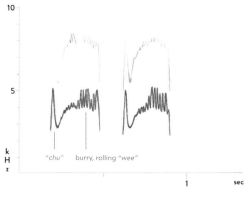

distinctive
"chuwee-chuwee"
song

"chu"   burry, rolling *"wee"*

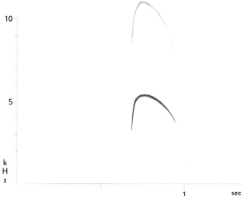

"peeur" call

RANGE AND HABITAT Resident of pine and broadleaf forests in the mountains and foothills of Mexico south through Central America. It is a very rare spring/summer visitor (has nested) to the mountains of southeast Arizona and west Texas. There is one spring record (April 22, 2014) on the central Texas coast. It moves to lower elevations in winter, where it can often be found in desert scrub and riparian habitats.

SIMILAR SPECIES Tufted Flycatcher is unlikely to be confused with any other flycatcher in the United States. Buff-breasted is of similar coloration, but it has a rounded crown.

TUFTED FLYCATCHER

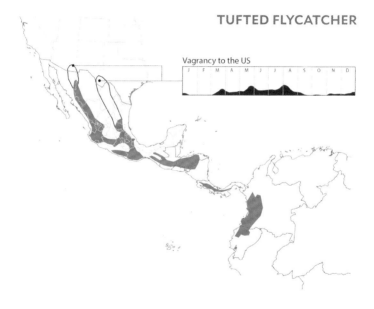

Vagrancy to the US

J F M A M J J A S O N D

Olive-sided Flycatcher
Contopus cooperi
L 7.0–7.9″ (18–20 cm), WT 1.1–1.3 oz (32–37 g)

GENERAL IDENTIFICATION Despite its name, the Olive-sided Flycatcher is a type of pewee. Crested appearance; long primary projection; stiff, relatively short and wide tail; and strongly contrasting open-vested appearance across breast and sides are diagnostic. When not obscured by wings, pair of white patches on sides of rump are uniquely diagnostic. Tail has a subtle fork. Underparts are whitish, contrasting strongly with dark, somewhat open vest and dark upperparts. Undertail coverts are often marked with dark chevrons or ventral streaks. Juvenal plumage is like adult. Olive-sided rarely flicks wings or tail. It usually perches motionless and erect on tall dead snags protruding from the forest canopy. Adult prebasic molt is complete and occurs on wintering grounds.

VOICE Olive-sided has a distinctive whistled song often described as "*quick-three-beers*." Call is a hollow sounding "*pip*," often given in threes. Individual "*pip*" is like that of the wood-pewees, but slightly lower in pitch.

RANGE AND HABITAT Olive-sided breeds in the coniferous forests of western North America north to Alaska and east across the Canadian boreal forest and into the northern Appalachians. It winters in northern South America and is found throughout much of the United States during migration. It is very rare in the United States during the winter (most winter records are from California). Spring migrants arrive in California and east to Texas in late Apr., continuing into late May. In interior mountains of the west, nesting birds may not arrive until late May. Fall migrants pass through southwestern United States from early Aug. to early Oct. While widespread during migration, they are not usually seen in large numbers. During breeding, it prefers forest edges with tall trees and snags.

SIMILAR SPECIES Olive-sided Flycatcher is unlikely to be confused with *Empidonax*. It can be confused with other *Contopus* species, but other pewees are uniformly dark across the chest/breast, have longer tails, and never have the open-vested appearance or whitish belly of Olive-sided.

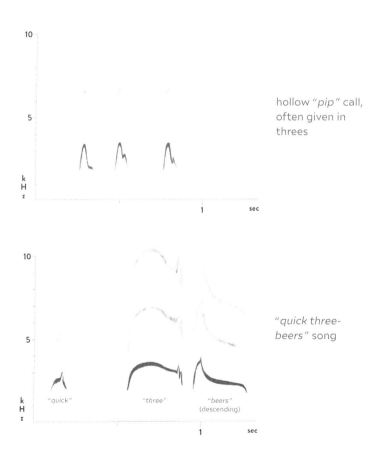

hollow "*pip*" call, often given in threes

"*quick three-beers*" song

"*quick*"   "*three*"   "*beers*" (descending)

OLIVE-SIDED FLYCATCHER

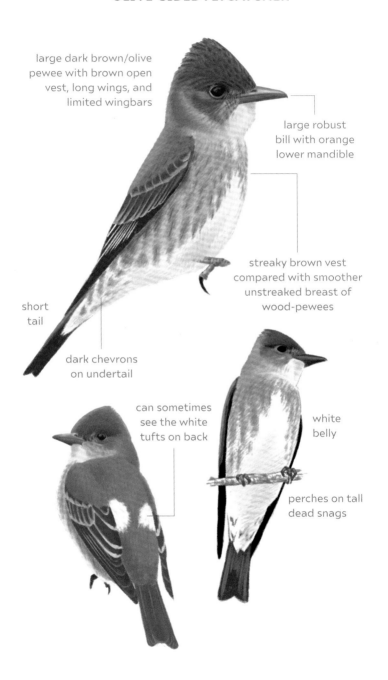

large dark brown/olive pewee with brown open vest, long wings, and limited wingbars

large robust bill with orange lower mandible

streaky brown vest compared with smoother unstreaked breast of wood-pewees

short tail

dark chevrons on undertail

can sometimes see the white tufts on back

white belly

perches on tall dead snags

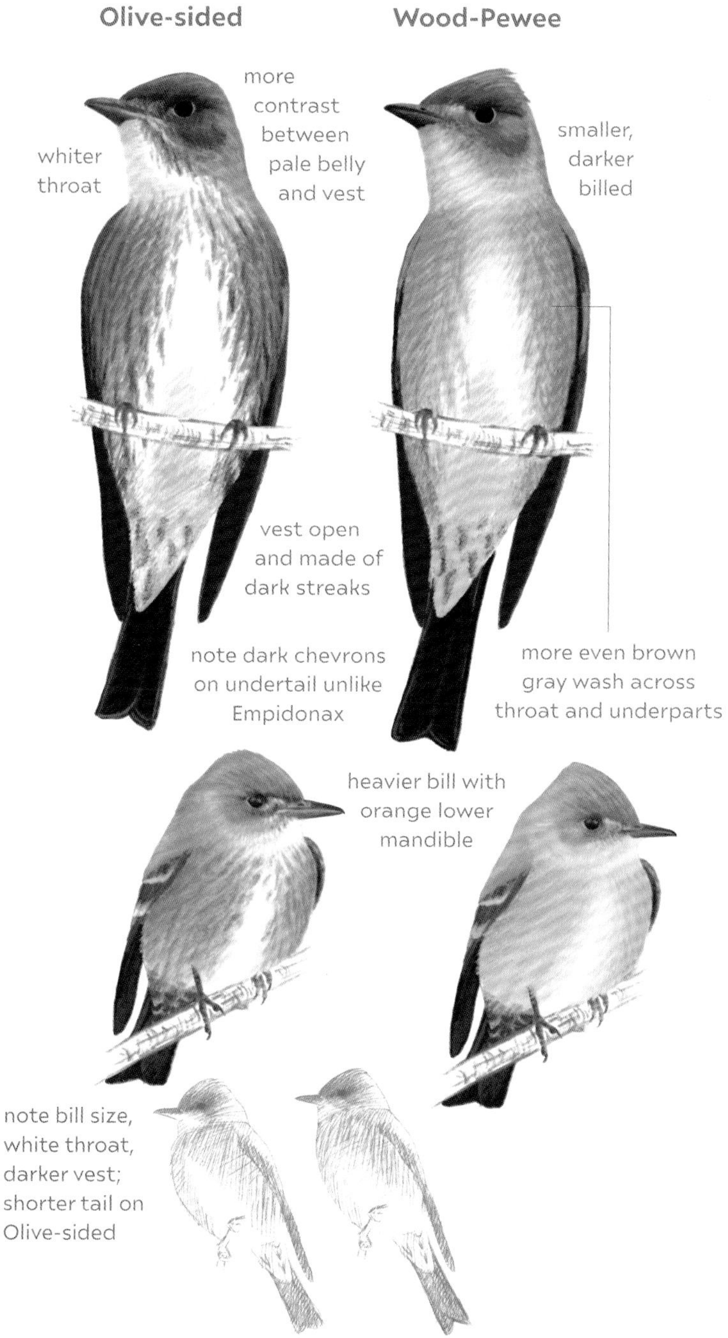

Olive-sided

Wood-Pewee

whiter throat

more contrast between pale belly and vest

smaller, darker billed

vest open and made of dark streaks

note dark chevrons on undertail unlike Empidonax

more even brown gray wash across throat and underparts

heavier bill with orange lower mandible

note bill size, white throat, darker vest; shorter tail on Olive-sided

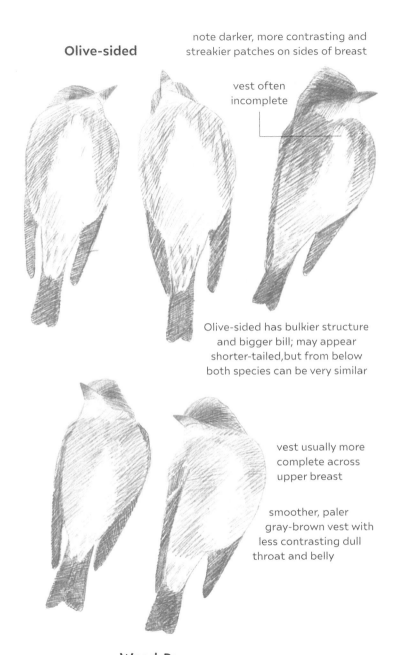

Olive-sided

note darker, more contrasting and streakier patches on sides of breast

vest often incomplete

Olive-sided has bulkier structure and bigger bill; may appear shorter-tailed, but from below both species can be very similar

vest usually more complete across upper breast

smoother, paler gray-brown vest with less contrasting dull throat and belly

Wood-Pewee

OLIVE-SIDED FLYCATCHER

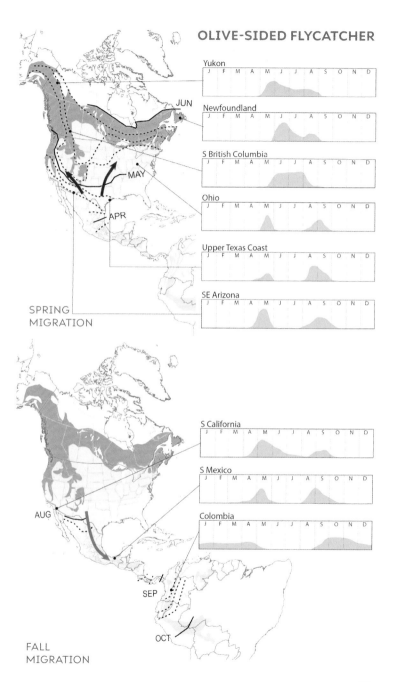

Yukon
J F M A M J J A S O N D

Newfoundland
J F M A M J J A S O N D

S British Columbia
J F M A M J J A S O N D

Ohio
J F M A M J J A S O N D

Upper Texas Coast
J F M A M J J A S O N D

SE Arizona
J F M A M J J A S O N D

JUN

MAY

APR

SPRING
MIGRATION

S California
J F M A M J J A S O N D

S Mexico
J F M A M J J A S O N D

Colombia
J F M A M J J A S O N D

AUG

SEP

OCT

FALL
MIGRATION

57

Greater Pewee
Contopus pertinax
L 7.1–8.0″ (18–20 cm), WT 0.95 oz (27 g)

GENERAL IDENTIFICATION Greater Pewee is usually unmistakable. It is a large, olive-colored pewee with a strongly pointed crest, long and heavy bill, completely orange lower mandible, and very long primary projection. Wingbars are dull. Chest is usually dark olive, resulting in weak upper/underpart contrast. It very rarely flicks wings or tail. It generally sits motionless on branches beneath the canopy, rarely above the canopy. Periodically sallies out for insects. Adult prebasic molt is complete and occurs on summering grounds.

VOICE Its distinctive song is a whistled repertoire consisting of a series of short "*perduit-perduit*" phrases and a distinctive drawn-out "*pew-pew-puWEEew*," often given the mnemonic "*Jose-Maria*." Its call is a single short "*pip*" or "*peeeur*" similar to that of wood-pewees, but at a slightly lower frequency and with a slightly hollower tone. It often calls at dawn.

RANGE AND HABITAT The Greater Pewee is resident in the mountains of Mexico and Central America. Between early Apr. and late Aug. its range expands into Arizona and locally to the Davis Mountains of west Texas for nesting. It is a rare winterer in the southwest from California to Texas and is the only expected winter pewee in the United States. It prefers middle story to upper canopy of pine and oak woodlands.

SIMILAR SPECIES Only wood-pewees are likely to be confused with Greater Pewee, but note Greater's longer bill, more pronounced crest, and longer tail.

GREATER PEEWEE

large, crested pewee with long
wings and orange lower mandible

long tail

long, heavy bill with
orange lower mandible

not vested
like Olive-sided
Flycatcher

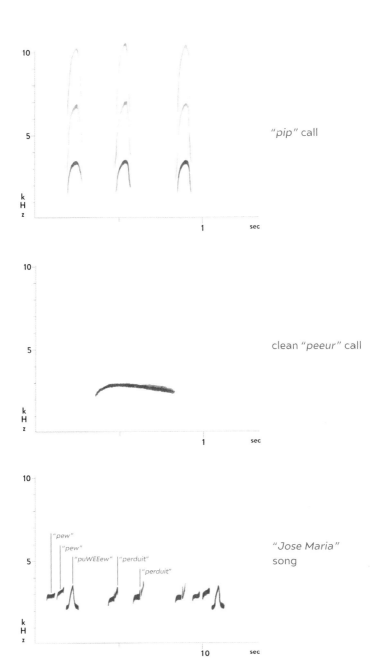

"pip" call

clean *"peeur"* call

"Jose Maria" song

"pew"
"pew"
"puWEEew" "perduit"
"perduit"

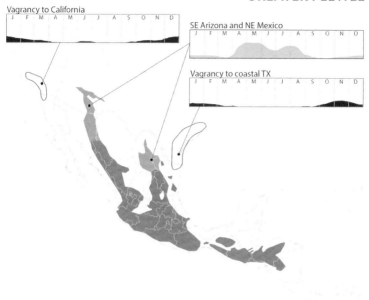

Vagrancy to California

SE Arizona and NE Mexico

Vagrancy to coastal TX

Western Wood-Pewee

Contopus sordidulus

L 6.25″ (15.9 cm), WT 0.46 oz (13 g)

Eastern Wood-Pewee

Contopus virens

L 6.25″ (15.9 cm), WT 0.49 oz (14 g)

GENERAL IDENTIFICATION Wood-pewees are separated from *Empidonax* by their slightly larger size, more slender and vertical posture, very long primary projection (saber-like), long bill, and wide tail. A combination of dark olive coloration, olive or dusky underparts, dull wingbars; inconspicuous or nonexistent eye-ring, presence of ventral streaks, and crested crown is diagnostic of wood-pewees. Wood-pewees rarely flick wings or tail. They often sit motionless on snags in or above the forest canopy. They tend to sally high and return to the same snag unlike *Empidonax* which often return to a different snag. Wood-pewees are often first detected by sound because they are highly vocal even during migration.

Visual identification of wood-pewees to species must be done with care and should be verified by voice whenever possible. Subtle plumage and structural differences may be used to hint at a possible out-of-range pewee. Western is darker, shows less contrast, and is subtly shorter tailed than Eastern. Slightly lighter underparts of Eastern give subtly stronger upper/underpart contrast than in Western. Both wood-pewees have dull wingbars, showing little contrast with upperparts. However, wingbars on Eastern can be slightly brighter than on Western. Upper and lower wingbars on Eastern are almost always of similar boldness or brightness, but on Western, the upper wingbar is usually duller than the lower wingbar.

Although there is overlap, Eastern tends toward a slightly shorter primary projection and a longer tail than Western: ratio of the primary projection (PP) to tail projection (TP) is greater in Western than in Eastern. Western tends to hold tail in line with its body and back, contributing to a straighter, more upright posture. Eastern often holds its tail slightly downward relative to its body, which, in combination with slightly more contrasting plumage, makes Eastern more reminiscent of an *Empidonax* than Western. Lower mandible is mostly orange in Eastern and dark in Western, but there is overlap. Neither species typically shows much of an eye-ring, but Eastern may occasionally show hint of an indistinct eye-ring. Both wood-pewees complete their prebasic molt on wintering grounds, although molt may begin on summering grounds. Some wood-pewees may be best left unidentified to species.

VOICE Pewee identification should consider all the above field marks collectively, but voice is the best way to be fully confident of an identification. Song of Eastern Wood-Pewee is a drawn-out slur "*PEE-a-weeeEEE*" with the last segment slightly rising. The Eastern Wood-Pewee song has a slight downward inflection in the middle of the phrase. Eastern Wood-Pewee call is a short "*pip*." Western Wood-Pewee song is shorter and burrier, a descending or rising "*BREeeer*." At dawn, the "*BREeeer*" phrase is often followed by a high-pitch twitter like that of Vermilion Flycatcher (*Pyrocephalus rubinus*). Western Wood-Pewee gives a short monotonic "*pee*" call. Both species call and sing often at dawn.

RANGE AND HABITAT
WESTERN WOOD-PEWEE Western Wood-Pewees breed in the coniferous mountains of western North America, from Alaska south through the Rocky Mountains and Coast Range to the Sierra Madre of Mexico. Western Wood-Peewees primarily winter in northwestern South America although small numbers may winter as far north as southern Mexico. They frequent the upper canopy of shaded woodlands, often perching on dead snags in or above the canopy. They are often found around riparian habitats. Northbound migrants

arrive in southern California and Arizona in mid-Apr. with late migrants continuing into early June. In fall, migrants pass through California and Arizona as early as late July and continue through the end of Sept. They arrive on South American wintering grounds from early Sept.; the last remaining winterers depart north by early May. It is very rare in the United States in winter.

EASTERN WOOD-PEWEE Eastern Wood-Pewees breed in deciduous and coniferous forests of eastern North America and winter in northwestern South America. They frequent the upper canopy of shaded woodlands, often on forest edges. Northbound migrants primarily take a circum-Gulf path through Texas with a smaller number cutting across the Gulf of Mexico from the Yucatan. A small number of spring migrants may transit through Florida by hopping the Caribbean islands. In fall, southbound migrants mostly reverse their spring migration routes, but a significant fraction migrates through Florida and across Cuba to reach Central America. Spring migrants arrive in the southern part of the United States by the second week of Apr. with migration continuing until the end of May. Arrival on northernmost breeding grounds is from early May. Southbound migrants reach Texas and Louisiana from mid-Aug., continuing to the end of Oct. with a few stragglers continuing into late Nov. Early Sept. is when the first birds arrive on wintering grounds with arrivals continuing into Nov. The last wintering birds depart their wintering grounds in Apr. It is very rare in the United States in winter.

SIMILAR SPECIES Olive-sided Flycatcher has more whitish ground color to underparts and has a shorter tail. Greater Pewee has a longer tail, much more pointed crest, and longer bill with completely orange lower mandible. Wood-pewees are often confused with dull-colored *Empidonax*, such as Willow, Alder, Hammond's, and Dusky. However, wood-pewees have much longer primary projection, stronger crest, and longer bill.

WESTERN WOOD-PEWEE

gray breast creates vested look

little to no eye-ring

indistinct upper wingbar

very long primary projection

bill longer than Empidonax, lower mandible mostly dark

dark streaks on undertail

peaked or crested crown

juveniles have buffier wingbars

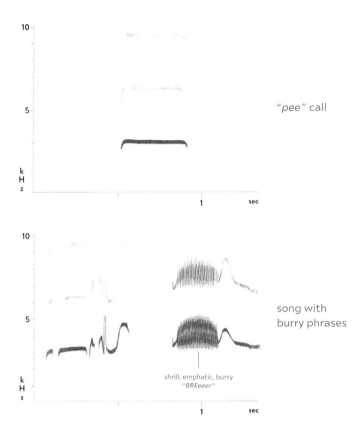

"*pee*" call

song with
burry phrases

shrill, emphatic, burry
"*BREeeer*"

WESTERN WOOD-PEEWEE

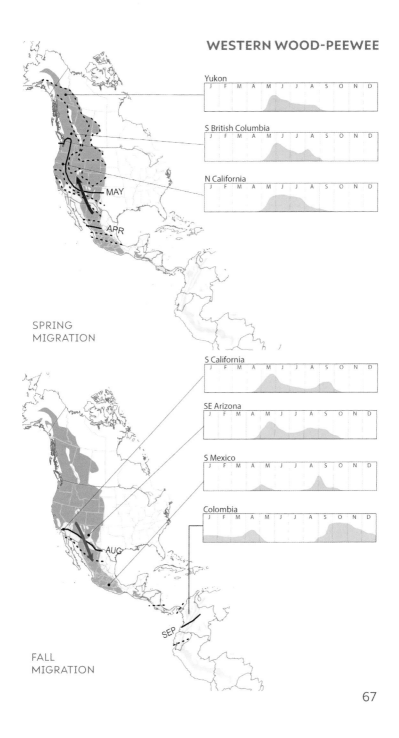

Yukon
S British Columbia
N California

SPRING
MIGRATION

MAY
APR

S California
SE Arizona
S Mexico
Colombia

AUG

SEP

FALL
MIGRATION

EASTERN WOOD-PEWEE

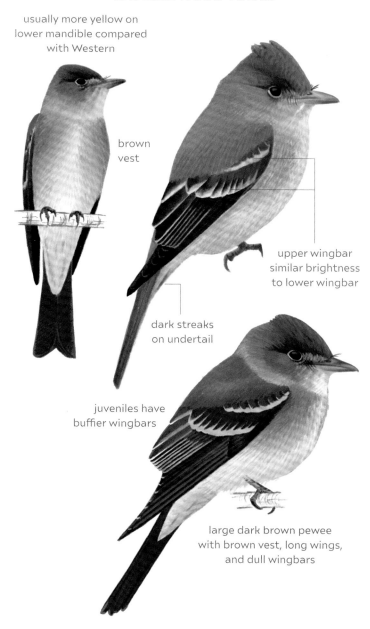

usually more yellow on
lower mandible compared
with Western

brown
vest

upper wingbar
similar brightness
to lower wingbar

dark streaks
on undertail

juveniles have
buffier wingbars

large dark brown pewee
with brown vest, long wings,
and dull wingbars

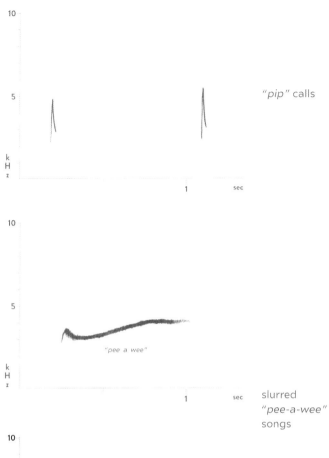

"*pip*" calls

"*pee a wee*"

slurred
"*pee-a-wee*"
songs

"PEE   a   weeeEEE"

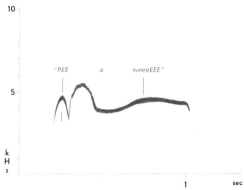

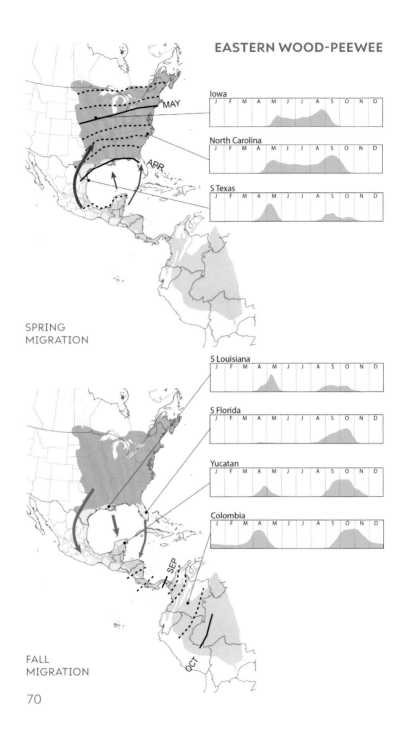

EASTERN WOOD-PEEWEE

Iowa
J F M A M J J A S O N D

North Carolina
J F M A M J J A S O N D

S Texas
J F M A M J J A S O N D

MAY

APR

SPRING
MIGRATION

S Louisiana
J F M A M J J A S O N D

S Florida
J F M A M J J A S O N D

Yucatan
J F M A M J J A S O N D

Colombia
J F M A M J J A S O N D

SEP

OCT

FALL
MIGRATION

Willow Flycatcher

Wood-Pewees

dull Willow has slightly
more complete eye-ring, paler
lores, brighter bill, and shorter primary
projection; lacks any dark chevrons
on the undertail

beware when looking up
at a pewee as primaries
can look shorter

Willow

Wood-Pewee

WOOD-PEWEES

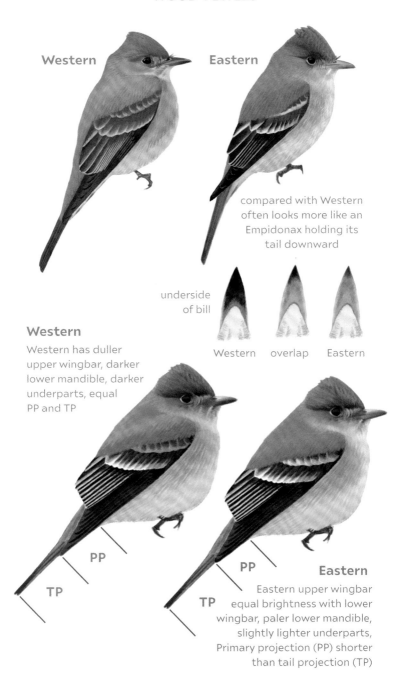

Western

Eastern

compared with Western
often looks more like an
Empidonax holding its
tail downward

underside
of bill

Western   overlap   Eastern

Western

Western has duller
upper wingbar, darker
lower mandible, darker
underparts, equal
PP and TP

PP

TP

PP

TP

Eastern

Eastern upper wingbar
equal brightness with lower
wingbar, paler lower mandible,
slightly lighter underparts,
Primary projection (PP) shorter
than tail projection (TP)

Cuban Pewee

Contopus caribaeus

L 5.9–6.5″ (15.0–16.5 cm), WT 0.30–0.48 oz (8.5–13.5 g)

GENERAL IDENTIFICATION The Cuban Pewee is a small flycatcher that frequents scrubby and open woodland habitats of the Bahamas and Cuba. Like other pewees, it has a long bill, peaked crown, dull wingbars, gray upperparts, and a yellowish suffusion to underparts. Its most distinctive feature is a bold, white postocular teardrop behind its eye, which contrasts strongly with the slaty gray face. It has the unusual habit, especially for a pewee, of flicking its tail upward once after landing.

VOICE Song is a high-pitch "*peee-WEE-oo*" or a high-pitch, descending slur, "*pip-PEEEEEuuur.*" Eastern Wood-Pewee's slurred song rises in pitch at the end, more like an up slur than the down slur of Cuban. Cuban call is a high-pitch "*pip*," like Eastern Wood-Pewee but higher in frequency.

RANGE AND HABITAT Cuban is a non-migratory resident of the Bahamas and Cuba, but it occasionally strays to the Florida Keys and the southeast coast of Florida in fall and spring. Strays occur when southerly or easterly winds prevail. Where resident, it is found from sea level to ~6,000 feet (1800 m) throughout a variety of habitats from broadleaf and pine forests to scrublands and mangroves.

SIMILAR SPECIES The Cuban Pewee is unlikely to be confused with *Empidonax* due to its dark coloration and lack of wingbars. It is most like the wood-pewees, but the white crescent behind eye, shorter primary projection and tail flicking after landing are unique. Cuban has no ventral streaks.

CUBAN PEWEE

long bill compared
with Eastern

eye-ring whitish
with postocular
teardrop

yellowish
suffusion to
underparts

no ventral
streaks

long primary
projection
compared with
Cuban Pewee

Eastern Wood-Pewee

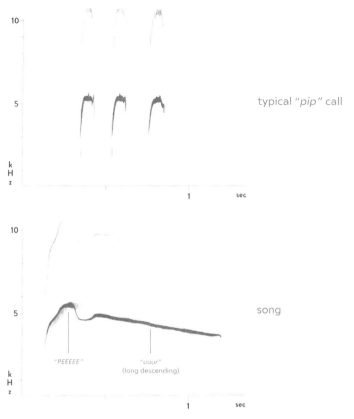

typical "*pip*" call

10
5
k
H
z

1   sec

10
5
k
H
z

"*PEEEEE*"   "*uuur*"
(long descending)

1   sec

song

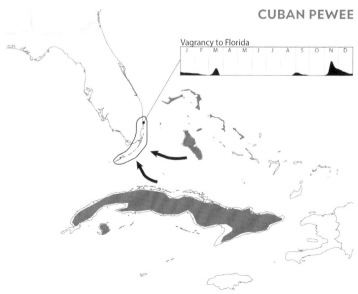

CUBAN PEWEE

Vagrancy to Florida

J F M A M J J A S O N D

Acadian Flycatcher

Empidonax virescens

L 5.75″ (14.6 cm), WT 0.46 oz (13 g)

GENERAL IDENTIFICATION The Acadian Flycatcher is phylogenetically the most unique *Empidonax*. It has the longest primary projection (appearing saber-like) of all *Empidonax*. On folded primaries, there are large gaps in the spacing of primary feather tips, accentuating the saber-like appearance. Its bill is longer than in other *Empidonax*. The lower mandible is always completely orange. Tail is of moderate length, but is the widest of all *Empidonax*, never narrowing toward the body. It often shows a peaked crown akin to Pacific-slope and Cordilleran but has the lowest forehead angle of all *Empidonax*. Chest and underparts are whitish, contrasting strongly with greenish upperparts. Wingbars are bold and contrast with black ground color of wing. Wing panel contrast is moderate. Pale edges on secondaries often approach closer to the lower wingbar, as in Pacific-slope and Cordilleran but unlike other *Empidonax*. Complete, bold, and crisp eye-ring is usually conspicuous. Lores are occasionally pale. Juvenal plumage is like adult's, but wingbars may have slight buffy tint. It is one of the more sedate *Empidonax*, often sitting motionless beneath the canopy for prolonged periods of time. Wing and tail flicking are less frequent than for other *Empidonax*. Adult Acadian completes prebasic molt on summering grounds, thus appearing fresh during fall migration.

VOICE Acadian gives a loud and explosive "*pwit-sip*" or downward "*peer*" song (often at dawn), often followed by a burst of short twitters and burry "*churrup*" notes. Its commonly heard call is a sharp, squeaky "*pweek*," which is at a higher frequency than the "*pip*" calls of pewees and most other *Empidonax*, but remarkably like the squeaky call of Yellow-bellied. It often emits a twittering call.

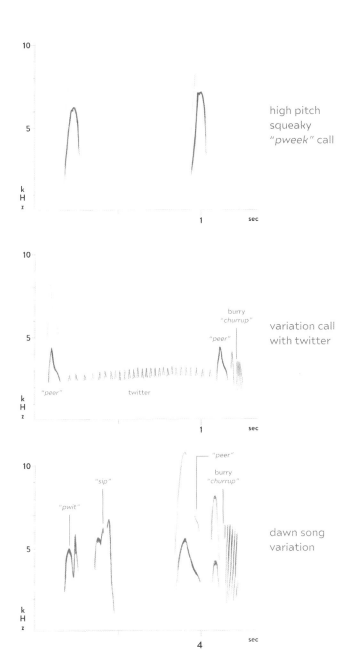

high pitch
squeaky
"pweek" call

variation call
with twitter

burry
"churrup"

"peer"

"peer"

twitter

dawn song
variation

"peer"

burry
"churrup"

"sip"

"pwit"

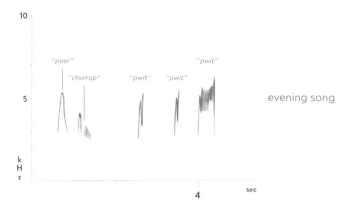

"peer"   "churrup"   "pwit"   "pwit"   "pwit"   evening song

10

5

k
H
z

4   sec

RANGE AND HABITAT Acadian is a summer resident of mature deciduous forests of the southeastern United States. It prefers mid-story and inner canopy of heavily shaded woodlands and bottomland forests, especially near streams or in swamps. It winters in northern South America and is virtually unrecorded in the United States in the winter and never as a vagrant to the Pacific coast. It is a strictly circum-Gulf migrant, traveling through Mexico and along the Texas coastline before dispersing across its eastern breeding grounds. Acadian is an early spring migrant, arriving during the first week of Apr., although migrants may continue passing through until late May. Fall migrants arrive on the Gulf coast by mid-Aug. and continue to the end of Sept. Birds wintering in northern South America arrive there by early Oct. and linger into Apr.

SIMILAR SPECIES Least has short primary projection, small bill, narrow tail, and typically messy eye-ring. Willow and Alder have medium primary projection, lower wingbar contrast, low wing panel contrast, nonexistent or thinner eye-ring, and less upper/underpart contrast compared with Acadian. Yellow-bellied has yellow chest, low upper/underpart contrast, smaller bill, and narrow tail. In Acadian, pale edges to secondary feathers more closely approach the lower wingbar than in Least and Yellow-bellied.

ACADIAN FLYCATCHER

shallow forehead

peaked
crown

strong
wing panel
contrast

crisp, bold
eye-ring

heavy bill

strong
upper/underpart
contrast

wide,
square-tipped
tail and long
primary
projection

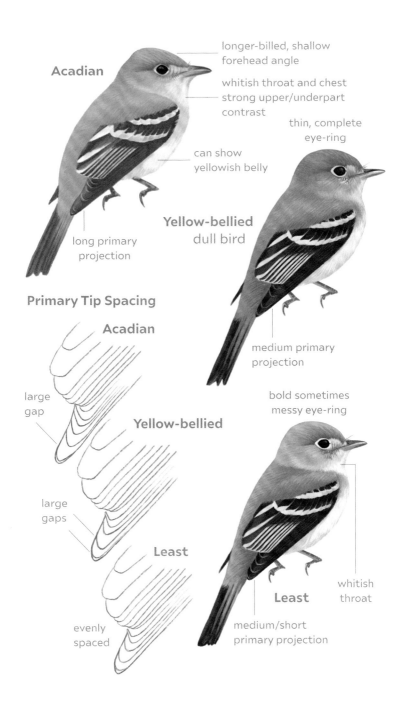

Acadian

longer-billed, shallow forehead angle

whitish throat and chest strong upper/underpart contrast

thin, complete eye-ring

can show yellowish belly

long primary projection

Yellow-bellied
dull bird

medium primary projection

Primary Tip Spacing

Acadian

large gap

Yellow-bellied

large gaps

Least

evenly spaced

bold sometimes messy eye-ring

whitish throat

Least

medium/short primary projection

ACADIAN FLYCATCHER

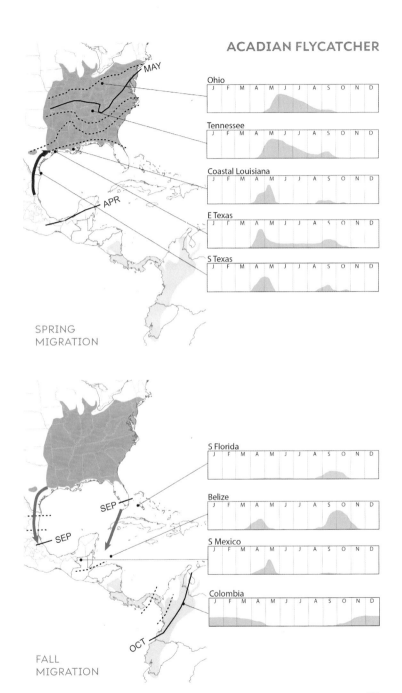

SPRING
MIGRATION

FALL
MIGRATION

Traill's Flycatchers

Willow *Empidonax traillii*
L 5.2–6.7″ (13.3–17.0 cm), WT 0.40–0.58 oz (11.3–16.4 g)

Alder *Empidonax alnorum*
L 5.1–6.7″ (13–17 cm), WT 0.42–0.49 oz (12–14 g)

GENERAL IDENTIFICATION The Traill's complex consists of Willow and Alder Flycatchers, historically considered to be conspecific and visually inseparable. Traill's differ from most of the other *Empidonax* by having slightly bulkier builds, medium-length bills, dull and less contrasting plumages, and medium-length tails. Traill's have an indistinct to nonexistent eye-ring (compared with other *Empidonax*), completely pale lower mandible, moderate wingbar contrast, moderate to strong wing panel contrast, moderate upper/underpart contrast, moderately wide tail, and medium primary projection. Traill's tend to have a more vertical posture with the tail often lining up with the back or only slightly tilted downward, superficially resembling the posture of pewees, especially in the case of Willow.

Identifying Traill's Flycatchers to species should be done with care and preferably confirmed by voice. Nevertheless, subtle plumage and structural differences exist. Alder has slightly more contrasting wingbars relative to wing and mantle. Alder also tends toward slightly darker upperparts and whiter chest than Willow, giving Alder slightly stronger upper/underpart contrast. Alder's crown is usually more rounded, whereas Willow can often show a subtle peak. Alder often displays a slightly steeper forehead angle, whereas Willow's is shallower. Eye-ring on Alder varies from nonexistent to very thin and crisp, and when present may contrast slightly with Alder's slightly darker face. In comparison with Alder, Willow's eye-ring can appear bolder but is more diffuse and messier, with less contrast against the lighter face of Willow. Molts of both species are completed on wintering grounds.

Brave birders may wish to explore differences between western (consisting of northwestern and southwestern forms) and eastern forms of Willow. Southwestern Willow tends toward being slightly grayer with duller wingbars than eastern forms, but more research is needed to resolve subspecific identification.

VOICE Willow and Alder both give burry songs, which can sound very similar to the untrained ear. However, with careful study, they can be separated. Willow's song is a sneezing two-syllable "*FITZ-brrrew*." Willow's song can be variable, but in nearly all cases, the first syllable "*FITZ*" is accented and rising, and the "*brrrew*" is more drawn out, burry, and descending. Southwestern forms of Willow have similar songs, but the descending "*brrrew*" phrase is distinctly more modulated than the eastern and northwestern forms. Alder's song, commonly given at dawn, is a "*free-BREER-o,*" but unlike Willow, the first syllable, "*free,*" of Alder's song is more monotonic and less rising than that of Willow, and the "*BREER-o*" has a more rising quality than the descending "*brrrew*" of Willow. Alder also gives a variety of less burry, more whistled songs after dawn, "*pwee*," "*pee-oo*," and "*zwee-oo*." Both species give short calls that are often diagnostic once other flycatchers are ruled out. Willow's call is a short, hollow "*whit*," like those of Gray and Dusky, but beginning at a lower frequency. Alder's call is a short, hollow, and monotonic "*pip*," more like that of Hammond's. Willow may occasionally give a variant of a call that sounds reminiscent of an Alder "*pip*." Although Willow's "*pip*" is longer and of lower frequency than Alder's, the two "*pip*" calls are best distinguished by analyzing spectrograms. Note that Alder does not give "*whit*" calls.

WILLOW FLYCATCHER

indistinct eye-ring,
pale lores

dull wingbars

medium to weak
upper/underpart
contrast

medium-width
tail

generally
paler than
Wood-Pewee

dull and thin eye-ring,
sloping forehead, often
slightly crested, and fairly
long bill; recalls Wood-Pewee

pale chested
compared with
pewee

WILLOW FLYCATCHER

Western

dull wingbars, short
to medium primary
projection

Eastern

slightly longer
primaries

brighter bird with
slightly whiter
wingbars

Alder Flycatcher

more rounded head shape,
shorter bill, more distinct eye-ring,
whiter wingbars, and stronger
wing panel contrast. May show
stronger upper/underpart contrast

Alder   **Willow**

ALDER FLYCATCHER

thin but crisp
eye-ring

medium wing
panel contrast

wide tail

medium primary
projection

round crown

ALDER FLYCATCHER

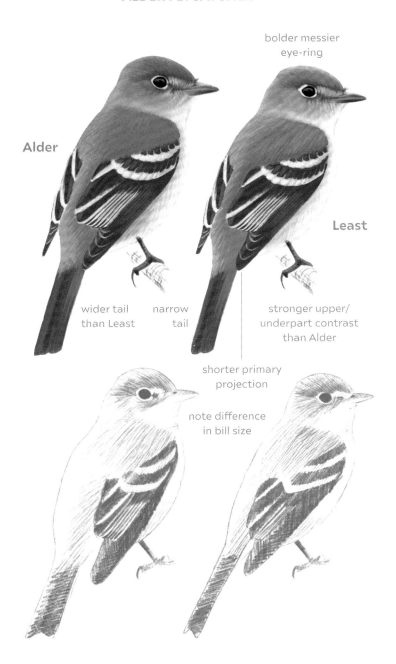

bolder messier
eye-ring

Alder

Least

wider tail
than Least

narrow
tail

stronger upper/
underpart contrast
than Alder

shorter primary
projection

note difference
in bill size

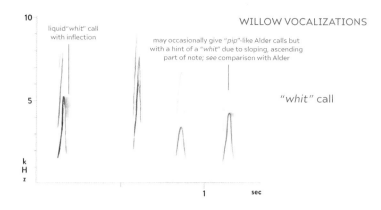

liquid "*whit*" call
with inflection

may occasionally give "*pip*"-like Alder calls but
with a hint of a "*whit*" due to sloping, ascending
part of note; *see* comparison with Alder

"*whit*" call

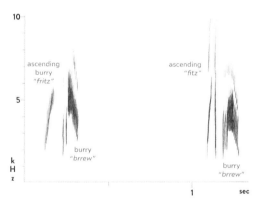

ascending
burry
"*fritz*"

burry
"*brrew*"

ascending
"*fitz*"

burry
"*brrew*"

"*fitz-brrew*"
songs

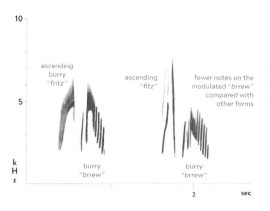

ascending
burry
"*fritz*"

burry
"*brrew*"

ascending
"*fitz*"

fewer notes on the
modulated "*brrew*"
compared with
other forms

burry
"*brrew*"

"*fitz-brrew*"
songs of
southwestern
forms of Willow

ALDER VOCALIZATIONS

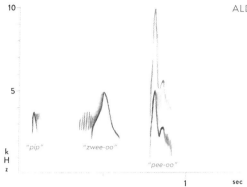

various calls,
most common
being the *"pip"*
call

"pip" *"zwee-oo"*

"pee-oo"

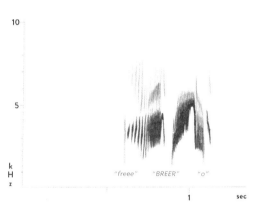

"freee-BREER-o"
dawn song

"freee" *"BREER"* *"o"*

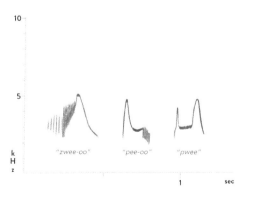

additional songs
and call notes

"zwee-oo" *"pee-oo"* *"pwee"*

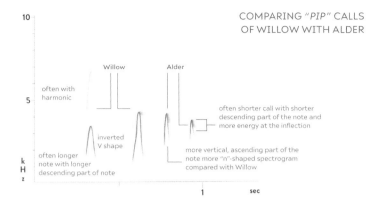

Willow   Alder

often with
harmonic

10

5

k
H
z

often shorter call with shorter
descending part of the note and
more energy at the inflection

inverted
V shape

more vertical, ascending part of the
note more "n"-shaped spectrogram
compared with Willow

often longer
note with longer
descending part of note

1   sec

RANGE AND HABITAT

WILLOW FLYCATCHER Willow breeds in shrubby riparian habitats
(often around willow thickets) throughout northeastern and western
United States. It winters from Central America to northwestern
South America. Willow is widespread in much of the United States
during migration but avoids Florida and other southeastern states. It
is very rare throughout the United States in winter, so any winter
record should be scrutinized. Willow is a late spring migrant. In the
west, Willow arrives in California from the second week of May, with
migrants continuing to pass through well into June. In the east,
Willow primarily arrives during the first week of May, with migrants
continuing through the third week of May. Reports of late Apr.
arrivals may need to be scrutinized. Fall migrants in the west return
through southern California and Arizona from late July to late Sept.
In the east, fall migrants arrive in Texas between mid-Aug. and
mid-Sept. Eastern fall migrants predominantly take a western
circum-Gulf route through Texas although small numbers go
through Florida in the fall, island hopping to Central America.

ALDER FLYCATCHER Alder breeds in boggy areas in the boreal
forests of Canada and northeastern United States. Alder winters in
the upper Amazonian basin in South America. It prefers brushy or

shrubby wetlands and woodland edges. It is often found in thickets of alders. Alder migrates primarily through the eastern United States. Spring migrants take a strictly western circum-Gulf route through Texas, arriving in the first week of May and continuing into late May. Alder is rare in spring east of Texas. Fall migration retraces the western circum-Gulf route, but part of the population takes a more easterly route through Louisiana and Florida. Fall migrants arrive in the southeastern United States by early Aug. and continue through late Sept. Birds first arrive on South American wintering grounds in Sept. Alder may commence spring and fall migration up to a week later than Willow, but more study is needed. There are no winter records of Alder in the United States. Spring and fall vagrants to California are very rare, though it is possible they are overlooked.

SIMILAR SPECIES The most similar species are Gray, Dusky, Acadian and Least Flycatchers, and wood-pewees. Gray has weak wing panel contrast, and narrow and longer tail. Dusky has smaller bill, more contrasting wingbars, and narrower tail. Acadian has longer primary projection, wider tail, bold eye-ring, strong wingbar contrast, and stronger wing panel contrast. Least has short and narrow tail, small bill, and strong wingbar and wing panel contrast. Least also has a strong upper/underpart contrast. Wood-pewees can be a source of confusion due to similar dull coloration, low wingbar contrast, vertical posture, and lack of wing and tail flicking. However, wood-pewees have much longer primary projection, longer bills, longer tails and darker chests. Note that Alder has slightly more contrasting overall plumage than Willow. Alder is very often confused with Least, while Willows, especially western forms of Willow, are often confused with wood-pewees.

WILLOW FLYCATCHER

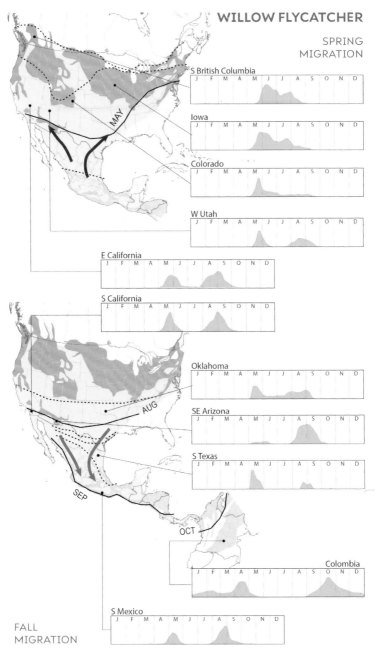

S British Columbia

J F M A M J J A S O N D

Iowa

J F M A M J J A S O N D

Colorado

J F M A M J J A S O N D

W Utah

J F M A M J J A S O N D

E California

J F M A M J J A S O N D

S California

J F M A M J J A S O N D

Oklahoma

J F M A M J J A S O N D

SE Arizona

J F M A M J J A S O N D

S Texas

J F M A M J J A S O N D

MAY

AUG

SEP

OCT

Colombia

J F M A M J J A S O N D

S Mexico

J F M A M J J A S O N D

FALL
MIGRATION

ALDER FLYCATCHER

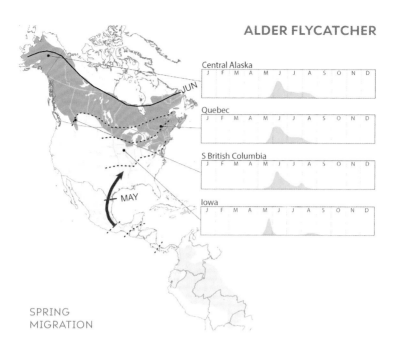

Central Alaska

Quebec

S British Columbia

Iowa

JUN

MAY

SPRING
MIGRATION

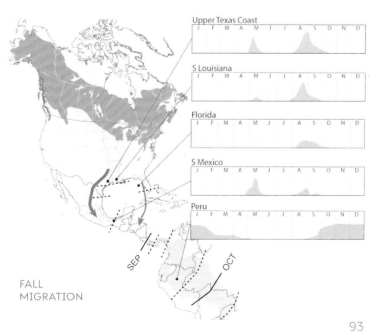

Upper Texas Coast

S Louisiana

Florida

S Mexico

Peru

SEP

OCT

FALL
MIGRATION

Yellow-bellied Flycatcher

Empidonax flaviventris

L 5.1–5.9″ (13–15 cm), WT 0.4 oz (11.5 g)

GENERAL IDENTIFICATION Yellow-bellied Flycatcher is a small flycatcher with a distinctive yellow-green overall coloration. Focus on the medium to long primary projection, bold and strongly contrasting wingbars relative to black wing color and mantle, and strong wing panel contrast (due to lack of pale edges to primary feathers). Eye-ring is complete, bold, and crisp. It has a medium-length bill with a completely pale lower mandible. Its tail is relatively short and narrow. Chest and underparts are greenish-yellow with weak upper/underpart contrast. Crown is round and forehead angle is moderate. Often observed flicking its wings and tail. Yellow-bellied is a shy bird, preferring shaded understory or inner canopy rather than open or shrubby areas on both breeding and wintering grounds. Adult molt is completed on wintering grounds.

VOICE Call is a sharp "*pip*," like Acadian, but higher than Hammond's. Commonly heard at dawn and dusk, its "*che-bunk*" song is very similar to the "*che-bek*" song of Least, but slightly longer and at a lower frequency. Yellow-bellied's "*che-bunk*" is also preceded by a very short "*pip*" that can be difficult to discern in the field, but in spectrograms is unlike Least. Yellow-bellied gives a "*pwee*" song at dusk, akin to that of wood-pewees but shorter.

RANGE AND HABITAT Yellow-bellied breeds in the boreal forests of the taiga from central Alaska east across Canada to Newfoundland. On breeding grounds it frequents spruce forests on the edges of bogs. It winters in Central America and migrates through eastern North America. Spring migrants primarily take a western circum-Gulf path through Texas, arriving in Texas no earlier than the first week of May. Northbound migrants then travel up the mid-continent, avoiding most of the southeastern United States (e.g., rare in Louisiana in spring). Arrives on breeding grounds in late May or even early June. Fall migration commences in the north in early Aug., but birds move quickly south, arriving on the Gulf coast and in Mexico by mid-Aug. Southbound migrants have a more easterly route, passing through Louisiana on their way down the Texas coast. A small number of southbound migrants transit through Florida and Cuba and possibly across the Gulf from Louisiana. It departs from wintering grounds in Central America in late Apr. It is a rare vagrant to the Pacific coast in late fall, but virtually unrecorded anywhere in the United States during winter.

SIMILAR SPECIES Least Flycatcher has a shorter primary projection than Yellow-bellied (note that the spacings between the outermost primary tips are wider than the inner primary tips, unlike the narrower, more even gaps in Least). Least's white throat also gives it a stronger upper/underpart contrast than Yellow-bellied. Least's eye-ring is messier or fuzzier. Acadian has longer bill, stronger upper/underpart contrast, and wider tail. Although ranges typically do not overlap, there is considerable confusion with Pacific-slope and Cordilleran during vagrancy. Teardrop-shaped eye-ring and crest of Pacific-slope and Cordilleran are diagnostic when apparent. Pacific-slope and Cordilleran have weak wing panel contrast because of pale edges to primary feathers; Yellow-bellied generally lacks pale edges to primary feathers. Note also that the pale edges to secondaries on Pacific-slope and Cordilleran extend closer to the lower wingbar than in Yellow-bellied.

YELLOW-BELLIED FLYCATCHER

yellow-green plumage, round crown, and bright wingbars
that contrast with black wings and greenish mantle

round crown

narrow tail

weak
upper/underpart
contrast

thin but bold, complete and
crisp eye-ring (sometimes
with hint of teardrop
shape)

strong wing panel
contrast

yellowish
underparts
variable

juveniles in fall with buffy
wingbars and vested look

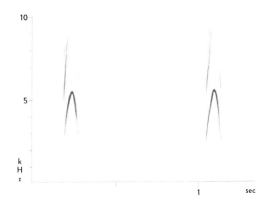

"pip" calls
similar to
Acadian
Flycatcher

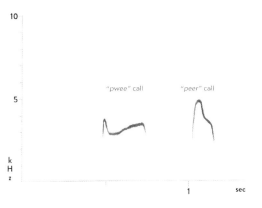

"pwee" call   "peer" call

"pwee" song
given at dusk

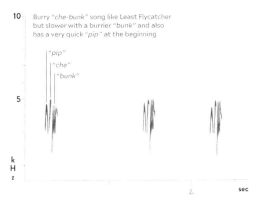

Burry *"che-bunk"* song like Least Flycatcher
but slower with a burrier *"bunk"* and also
has a very quick *"pip"* at the beginning

"pip"
"che"
"bunk"

burry
"che-bunk"
song given
at dawn

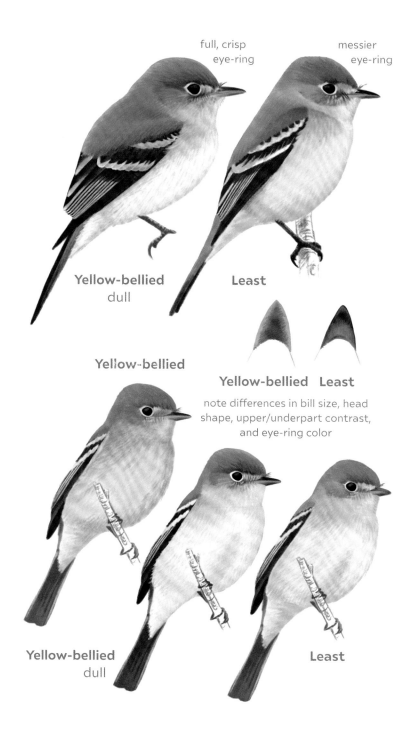

full, crisp
eye-ring

messier
eye-ring

Yellow-bellied
dull

Least

Yellow-bellied

Yellow-bellied **Least**

note differences in bill size, head
shape, upper/underpart contrast,
and eye-ring color

Yellow-bellied
dull

Least

Pacific-slope
weak wing
panel contrast

Yellow-bellied
strong wing
panel contrast

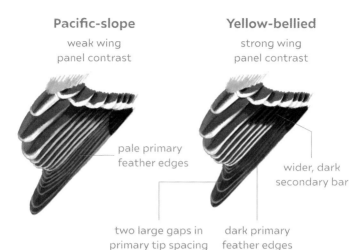

pale primary
feather edges

wider, dark
secondary bar

two large gaps in
primary tip spacing

dark primary
feather edges

Pacific-slope
peaked crown

Yellow-bellied
rounded crown

note differences in
head shape and eye-ring

YELLOW-BELLIED FLYCATCHER

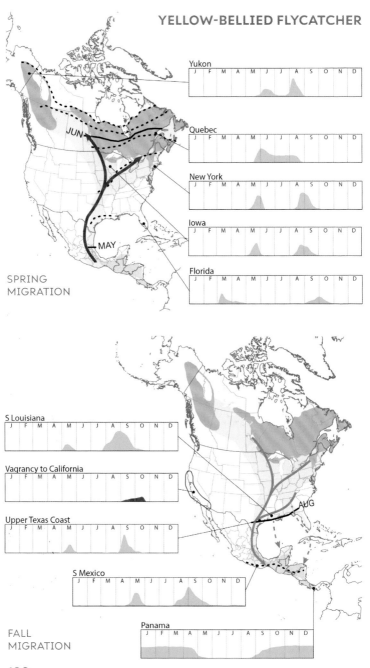

Yukon

Quebec

New York

Iowa

Florida

SPRING
MIGRATION

S Louisiana

Vagrancy to California

Upper Texas Coast

S Mexico

Panama

FALL
MIGRATION

Western Flycatcher

Pacific-slope *Empidonax difficilis*
L 5.5″ (14 cm), WT 0.39 oz (11 g)

Cordilleran *Empidonax occidentalis*
L 5.5″ (14 cm), WT 0.39 oz (11 g)

GENERAL IDENTIFICATION   Pacific-slope and Cordilleran
Flycatchers are usually unmistakable due to their overall greenish-
yellow coloration, distinctive crest, and teardrop-shaped eye-ring.
Confusion can occur with dull birds or when the crest is temporarily
flattened, but combination of medium-length bill, completely orange
lower mandible, medium to long primary projection, narrow tail,
relatively bold wingbars, weak wing panel contrast, and weak upper/
underpart contrast are diagnostic. Weak wing panel contrast is due to
very distinct pale edges to the primaries and secondaries. Pale edges
of secondaries usually continue up to or close to the lower wingbars,
unlike in most other *Empidonax*. Both Flycatchers habitually flick
their wings and tail. Juvenal plumage is like adult, but wingbars often
have buffier tone. Molt is mostly completed on wintering grounds.

The two species are treated together here as "Western" Flycatcher
because they are almost indistinguishable and may in fact represent
one species complex due to continuous gradation in plumage and
vocalizations where their ranges overlap. At the extremes, subtle
differences are worth noting. On average, Cordilleran has a slightly
heavier bill than Pacific-slope. Cordilleran's upper mandible may
also have a slightly more pronounced hook at its tip. The pale feather
edging of the primaries in Cordilleran is generally bolder than in
Pacific-slope, giving Cordilleran an especially weak wing panel
contrast. The wingbars on Cordilleran may also tend toward being
more yellowish and more concolorous with the mantle, resulting
in weaker wingbar-mantle contrast. In Pacific-slope, the wingbars
are slightly whiter, resulting in a stronger wingbar-mantle contrast.

However, there is a continuous spectrum where their breeding ranges approach. Extralimital birds should be referred to as Western Flycatchers if vocalizations are not recorded or if vocalizations are intermediate in character.

VOICE Although voice is the only robust way to separate the two species of Western Flycatchers, only at the extremes is song reliable. Where their breeding ranges meet, songs and calls fall within a continuous spectrum between the two species. Pacific-slope gives a rising, up-slurred "*PE-u-WEEET*" call with a slight downward inflection in the middle. Cordilleran gives a similar rising two-note "*chew-wit*," but without a downward inflection. The last note in Cordilleran is shorter and more abrupt than the last note of Pacific-slope's call. Both species also give high "*tseet*" calls reminiscent of a titmouse. Songs of both species consist of a series of various call notes but without any burry phrases like other western *Empidonax*. Because of geographic gradation in calls, out-of-range birds that are silent should be left unidentified.

RANGE AND HABITAT
PACIFIC-SLOPE FLYCATCHER Pacific-slope breeds in lowland deciduous to coniferous forests along the Pacific coast from northern Baja California north to British Columbia and winters in coastal Mexico, including Baja California. Spring migrants arrive on southern California breeding grounds by mid-Mar. and in British Columbia by mid-May. They depart from breeding grounds in late July. Southbound migrants arrive at coastal and desert migratory stopovers in southwestern United States from late July to early Aug. Birds wintering in southern Mexico arrive by mid-Oct. and stay until early Mar., with some lingering into Apr. Pacific-slope is a rare but regular stray to the Gulf Coast and eastern North America in late fall and winter. On both breeding and wintering grounds, Pacific-slope is found in shaded microhabitats, preferring the understory or inner canopy.

CORDILLERAN FLYCATCHER Cordilleran breeds at higher elevations than Pacific-slope, in the dry forests of the Rocky Mountains and Sierra Madre of Mexico and is a year-round resident in the latter. Northern breeding range of Cordilleran reaches eastern Washington, Idaho, and western Montana, where vocalizations begin to overlap with those of Pacific-slope. Winters in Mexico and along the Pacific coast of Mexico, but absent from Baja California. Cordilleran migrates primarily through the Basin and Range of Nevada with birds passing through west Texas as early as mid-Apr. and through Arizona by late Apr., later than Pacific-slope. Spring migration continues through late May. Southbound migrants appear in migratory stopover sites by late July and into late Sept. Cordilleran is probably a rare but regular stray to the Gulf Coast, but status is currently unclear. Like Pacific-slope, Cordilleran is found on breeding and wintering grounds in shaded microhabitats.

SIMILAR SPECIES Often confused with Yellow-bellied due to similar coloration. Yellow-bellied has a rounder crown, only rarely showing a subtle peak and never a crest (although Pacific-slope and Cordilleran can occasionally show round crown). Yellow-bellied's eye-ring is usually of uniform thickness but beware of Pacific-slope and Cordilleran occasionally showing a reduced tear. When eye-ring shape is inconclusive, focus on the wings. Yellow-bellied shows strong wing panel contrast and Pacific-slope and Cordilleran weak contrast. The extent to which the pale edges on secondary feathers extend up along the wing also differs. Pale secondary edges do not continue all the way to the lower wingbars in Yellow-bellied, resulting in a wide vertical, dark stripe in Yellow-bellied's folded secondary stack. In Pacific-slope and Cordilleran, pale feather edges of the secondaries extend closer to or even meet the lower wingbars. Dull Pacific-slope and Cordilleran can be confusing. In such birds, focus on relative contrast of wingbars and wing panel as well as structural features.

PACIFIC-SLOPE VOCALIZATIONS

"PE-u-WEEET" call with terminal frequency generally higher than Cordilleran, but note geographic variation and overlap

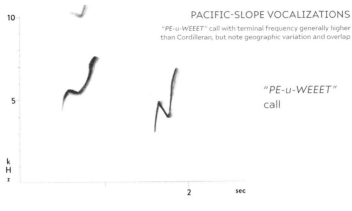

"PE-u-WEEET"
call

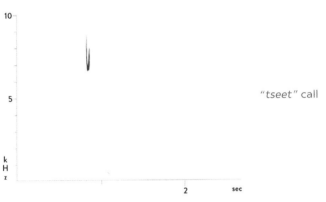

"tseet" call

Dawn song (sometimes during day). Three phrases repeated over. No burry notes like other western empids

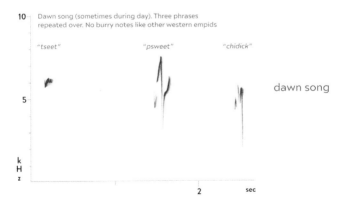

dawn song

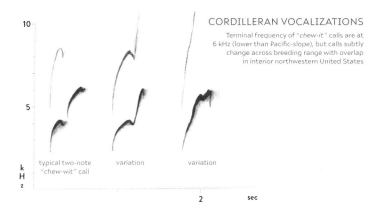

CORDILLERAN VOCALIZATIONS

Terminal frequency of "*chew-it*" calls are at 6 kHz (lower than Pacific-slope), but calls subtly change across breeding range with overlap in interior northwestern United States

typical two-note "*chew-wit*" call   variation   variation

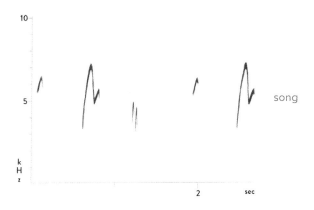

song

variation in calls from west to east (California to Colorado)

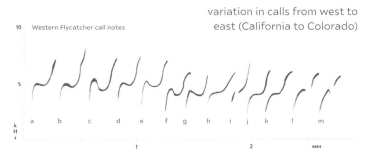

Western Flycatcher call notes

a. Pacific-slope, SE California
b. Pacific-slope, SW Arizona
c. Pacific-slope, W Oregon
d. Pacific-slope, coastal California
e. Pacific-slope, coastal slope Sierras, California
f. Pacific-slope, Alberta
g. Pacific-slope, W British Columbia

h. presumed Pacific-slope, E Washington
i. presumed Cordilleran, E Washington
j. presumed Cordilleran, S Alberta
k. presumed Cordilleran, Montana
l. Cordilleran, Colorado
m. Cordilleran, SE Arizona

PACIFIC-SLOPE FLYCATCHER

bold wingbars but often similar color to upperparts

peaked crown

teardrop-shaped eye-ring

weak upper/underpart contrast

weak wing panel contrast (pale edges to primary feathers)

Fall juveniles with buffy wingbars and duller underparts

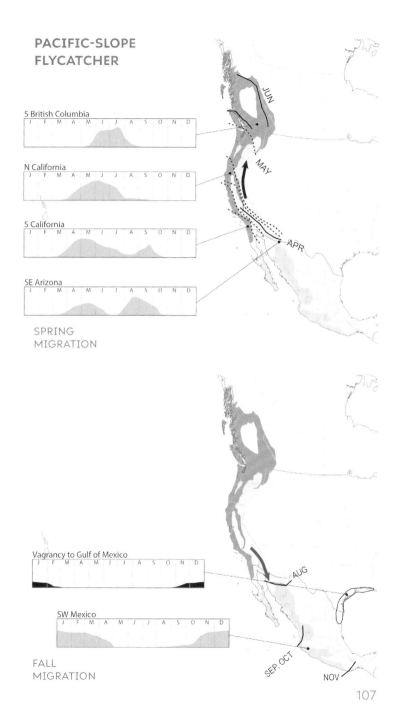

PACIFIC-SLOPE
FLYCATCHER

S British Columbia
J F M A M J J A S O N D

N California
J F M A M J J A S O N D

S California
J F M A M J J A S O N D

SE Arizona
J F M A M J J A S O N D

SPRING
MIGRATION

JUN

MAY

APR

Vagrancy to Gulf of Mexico
J F M A M J J A S O N D

SW Mexico
J F M A M J J A S O N D

FALL
MIGRATION

AUG

SEP, OCT

NOV

CORDILLERAN FLYCATCHER

nearly identical to Pacific-slope, but may appear slightly greener overall with slightly weaker wing panel contrast. In general, not identifiable without hearing vocalization

CORDILLERAN FLYCATCHER

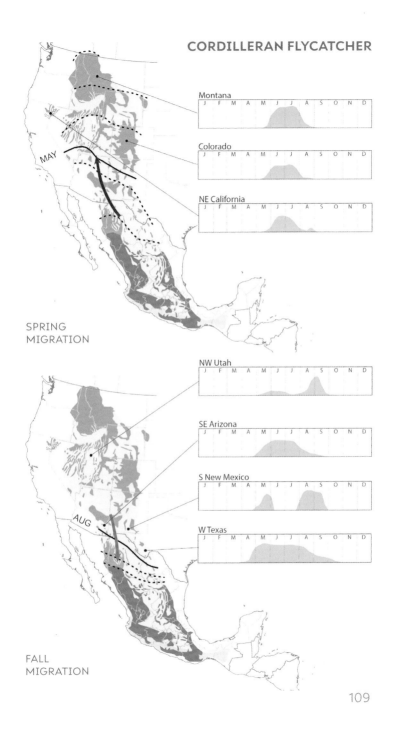

Montana

Colorado

NE California

MAY

SPRING
MIGRATION

NW Utah

SE Arizona

S New Mexico

W Texas

AUG

FALL
MIGRATION

Hammond's Flycatcher
Empidonax hammondii
L 4.9–5.7″ (12.5–14.5 cm), WT 0.27–0.43 oz (7.7–12.1 g)

GENERAL IDENTIFICATION Hammond's is a small and compact *Empidonax* with a small bill, proportionately large head, and dark olive-gray overall coloration. Combination of dark coloration and long primary projection is diagnostic. Large-headed appearance is accentuated by round crown and steep forehead angle, the steepest of all *Empidonax*. Lower mandible is usually all dark. Hammond's often appears short-tailed because of its long primary projection. Tail is narrow and often slightly forked. Both the chest and throat are dark with little contrast with equally dark upperparts. Wing ground color tends to be dark (but not black), resulting in medium wingbar contrast. Wing panel contrast is medium to strong. Eye-ring is generally conspicuous, but boldness and shape is variable. Hammond's often flicks wings and tail. Prebasic molt completed on summering grounds, so birds in fall migration look fresh.

VOICE Hammond's gives a two-note "*PIT-tic*" song, commonly at dawn, with second note short and abrupt. Dawn songs also include variants of short two-note burry phrases (Dusky has only one burry phrase in its song). Dawn songs often given in rapid succession at a rate of slightly more than one per second (Dusky is slower paced). Hammond's also gives a clear "*peeo*" and "*peace-out*" song, the latter like Dusky. Calls are a short "*pip*" or "*peek*" like Alder. Commonly heard "*pip*" call sounds monotonic compared with the rising "*whit*" of Willow, Least, and Dusky. Hammond's does not "*whit*."

RANGE AND HABITAT Hammond's breeds in the mountains of the west, from California north to central Alaska. It prefers cool coniferous forests, especially with fir (up to timberline). It winters primarily in similar habitats in the mountains of Central America. It is rare in winter in the United States except in southeastern Arizona and southern Texas, where small numbers regularly winter. In migration, found in a variety of habitats, including open, shrubby, and wooded areas.

Spring migrants arrive in southern California and the southwestern deserts from late Mar. to early Apr. with migrants continuing into mid- to late May. They arrive on the southern parts of the breeding range in late Apr. and on the northernmost parts in early May. Arrival in northwestern part of range is earlier than for those breeding in the continental interior. They commence southbound migration in late June to early July with most departing from breeding grounds by late July to early Aug. Fall migrants in the desert southwest arrive in early Aug. and peak in late Aug. through early Sept. with most passing through by late Sept. to early Oct. Wintering birds arrive in central Mexico in mid-Sept. and stay no longer than early Apr. They are rare but regular strays to the eastern United States in late fall and winter.

SIMILAR SPECIES Least has white chest/throat, strong upper/underpart contrast, all pale lower mandible, short primary projection, stronger wingbar contrast, and stronger wing panel contrast. Dusky has a slightly longer bill, short to medium primary projection, shallower forehead angle, moderate wingbar contrast, and weak wing panel contrast. Dusky is also slightly longer tailed than Hammond's. Dusky's tail is usually less forked than Hammond's. Dusky's lower mandible tends to range from a dull orange base to fully orange. Gray has much longer tail, longer bill, weak wingbar and wing panel contrast, and completely orange lower mandible. Occasionally, Hammond's is confused with Western Wood-Pewee due to similar dark coloration, but wingbars of Hammond's are distinctly bolder than those of wood-pewees. Wood-pewees also have much longer saber-like wings and wider tails.

HAMMOND'S FLYCATCHER

small, dull olive-gray western empid with steep forehead angle and small bill

gray chest and throat

bolder eye-ring than Dusky

weak upperpart/underpart contrast

long primary projection and short tail

dull yellow-green underparts

medium wingbar contrast

mostly to almost all dark lower mandible

medium wing panel contrast

some winter birds can be dull

forked tail

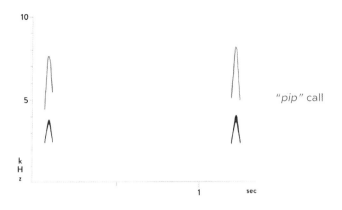

"pip" call

Dawn song consists of three short phrases given in rapid succession. Note two burry phrases, unlike Dusky, which has only one burry phrase in its song

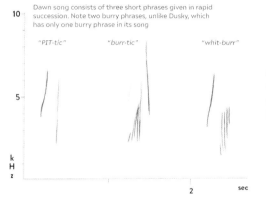

"PIT-tic"   "burr-tic"   "whit-burr"

songs composed
of various call
phrases given
in succession

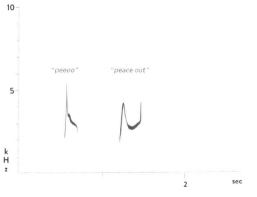

"peeoo"   "peace out"

other rapid
call notes

113

HAMMOND'S FLYCATCHER

brighter, yellowish individual

Hammond's

Dusky

long primary projection and shorter tail

shorter primary projection and longer tail

tail often more forked than Dusky

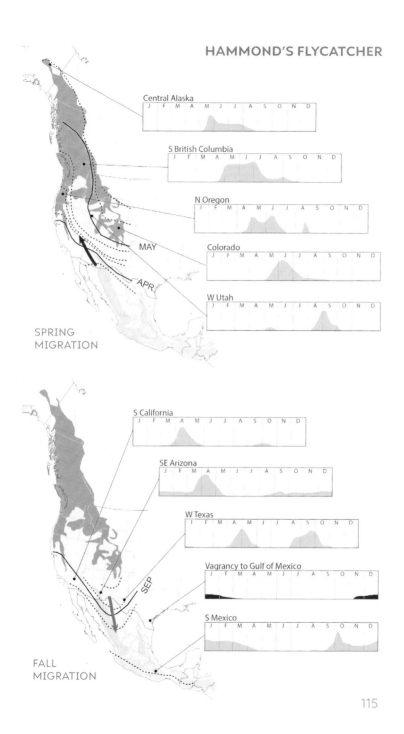

HAMMOND'S FLYCATCHER

Central Alaska
J F M A M J J A S O N D

S British Columbia
J F M A M J J A S O N D

N Oregon
J F M A M J J A S O N D

Colorado
J F M A M J J A S O N D

W Utah
J F M A M J J A S O N D

MAY

APR

SPRING
MIGRATION

S California
J F M A M J J A S O N D

SE Arizona
J F M A M J J A S O N D

W Texas
J F M A M J J A S O N D

Vagrancy to Gulf of Mexico
J F M A M J J A S O N D

S Mexico
J F M A M J J A S O N D

SEP

FALL
MIGRATION

Dusky Flycatcher

Empidonax oberholseri

L 5.1–6″ (13–15.2 cm), WT 0.32–0.40 oz (9.3–11.4 g)

GENERAL IDENTIFICATION Dusky is a small, slender flycatcher with overall light gray/olive plumage, medium-length tail, short to medium primary projection, round crown, and intermediate forehead angle. It has a short- to medium-length bill. Lower mandible is mostly dark with a pale base, but in poor light lower mandible can often look completely dark. Chest, throat, and upperparts are light gray, resulting in weak upper/underpart contrast. Wingbars are off-white to light gray, resulting in medium to weak wingbar contrast with upperparts and dusky gray base color of the wings. Whitish fringes to primary feathers result in weak wing panel contrast. Eye-ring is distinct but often diffuse and messy, resulting in medium to weak contrast with grayish face. Dusky often shows pale lores, though other *Empidonax* can also show pale lores. Like other *Empidonax*, Dusky habitually flicks its wings. It pumps its tail in a continuous fashion rather than the more intermittent flicking of other *Empidonax*. Such tail pumping is reminiscent of Gray Flycatcher, but respective speeds of up and down strokes in Dusky are similar. Dusky forages low in vegetation rather than from the tops of trees. Prebasic molt begins on summering grounds but is completed on wintering grounds.

VOICE Most common call is a short rising "*whit*," distinctly different from "*pip*" of Hammond's but very similar to Gray, Least, and Willow calls. Dusky's "*whit*" spectrogram is longer and shows a more upward inflection than Gray. Dusky's "*whit*" covers a slightly higher frequency range and lacks the energetic harmonic of Least. Frequent two-note "*PIT-tic*" dawn song is like that of Hammond's but given in only brief successions with prolonged pauses between. Other dawn songs are also of two notes like Hammond's, but typically ending with a burry or clear up slur instead of a down slur. Diurnal song is a two-note whistled "*bean-dip*," often given in conjunction with "*whit*" call notes.

RANGE AND HABITAT Dusky breeds in open coniferous forests, chaparral habitats and scrubby riparian areas in the mountains and foothills of the American west from the Transverse Ranges in southern California and the Colorado Plateau in Arizona north to northwestern Canada. It winters in the southwestern United States south to Mexico. Spring migrants pass through the southwestern United States from late Mar. to early Apr. and continue into late May. Fall birds depart breeding grounds in July and arrive at southwestern United States stopover sites by early Aug. Arrives in central Mexico wintering grounds by early Sept. with the last wintering individuals departing to the north by early May. Like Gray, Dusky avoids the immediate coast during migration, preferring interior mountains or deserts. It is a rare stray to the Gulf Coast and eastern United States in late fall and winter.

SIMILAR SPECIES In the west, most likely to be confused with Hammond's. Hammond's has longer primary projection, proportionately shorter tail, stronger wing panel contrast, stronger wingbar contrast, darker chest and overall coloration, and a steep forehead angle. The bill of Hammond's is smaller and usually all dark, but there is overlap in bill size. The pale base of Dusky's lower mandible can often be dusky and difficult to discern. Gray is similar in overall color, but with longer bill and tail. Gray tends to drop tail slowly after flicking it upward, whereas Dusky pumps tail up and down at equal rates. Brightly colored Dusky can look very much like Least, while dull-colored Least can look like Dusky. Least has a stronger wing panel and wingbar contrast, stronger upper/underpart contrast (throat white in Least and gray in Dusky), and proportionately shorter tail. Least's "*whit*" call is sharper and more emphatic than Dusky's more liquid "*whit*."

DUSKY FLYCATCHER

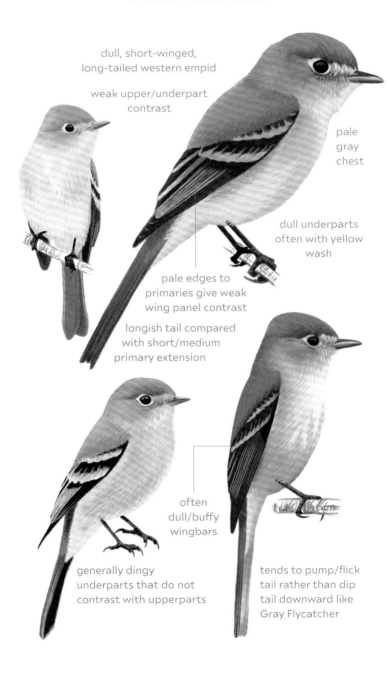

dull, short-winged, long-tailed western empid

weak upper/underpart contrast

pale gray chest

dull underparts often with yellow wash

pale edges to primaries give weak wing panel contrast

longish tail compared with short/medium primary extension

often dull/buffy wingbars

generally dingy underparts that do not contrast with upperparts

tends to pump/flick tail rather than dip tail downward like Gray Flycatcher

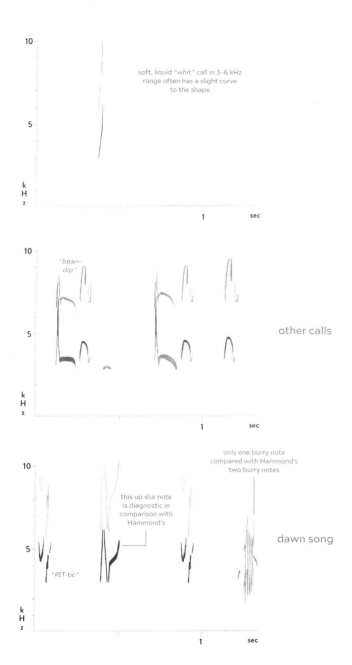

soft, liquid *"whit"* call in 3–6 kHz range often has a slight curve to the shape

"*bean-dip*"

other calls

only one burry note compared with Hammond's two burry notes

this up slur note is diagnostic in comparison with Hammond's

dawn song

"*PIT-tic*"

DUSKY FLYCATCHER

Dusky

winter birds variably dull
and yellowish below

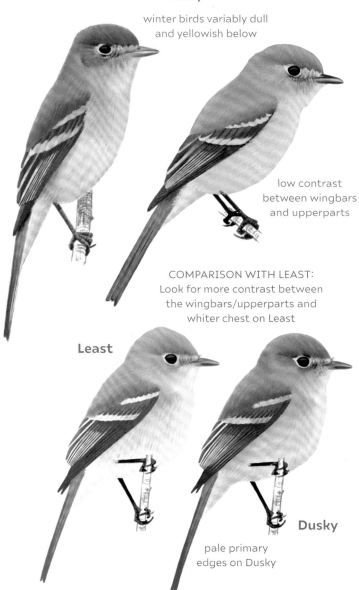

low contrast
between wingbars
and upperparts

COMPARISON WITH LEAST:
Look for more contrast between
the wingbars/upperparts and
whiter chest on Least

Least

Dusky

pale primary
edges on Dusky

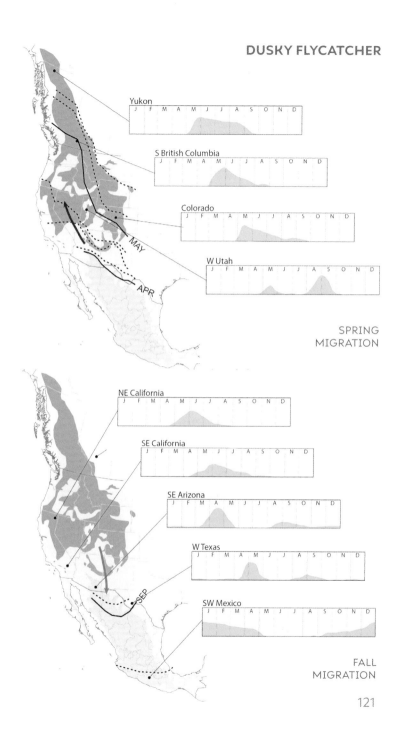

DUSKY FLYCATCHER

Yukon
J F M A M J J A S O N D

S British Columbia
J F M A M J J A S O N D

Colorado
J F M A M J J A S O N D

W Utah
J F M A M J J A S O N D

MAY

APR

SPRING
MIGRATION

NE California
J F M A M J J A S O N D

SE California
J F M A M J J A S O N D

SE Arizona
J F M A M J J A S O N D

W Texas
J F M A M J J A S O N D

SW Mexico
J F M A M J J A S O N D

SEP

FALL
MIGRATION

COMPARISON OF HAMMOND'S, DUSKY, GRAY AND LEAST FLYCATCHERS

Dusky

medium/short primary projection; relatively longer tail

weak wing panel contrast

Hammond's

steep forehead   smaller bill

bolder wingbars

plumage can be identical so focus on structure, habits, and call. Some silent birds may best be left unidentified

darker chest than Dusky

long primary projection; relatively short tail

long bill with yellowish lower mandible

very weak wing panel contrast

Gray

medium/short primary projection; long tail

Gray often dips tail down in deliberate fashion. Dusky and Hammond's nervously flick wings and flick/pump tail

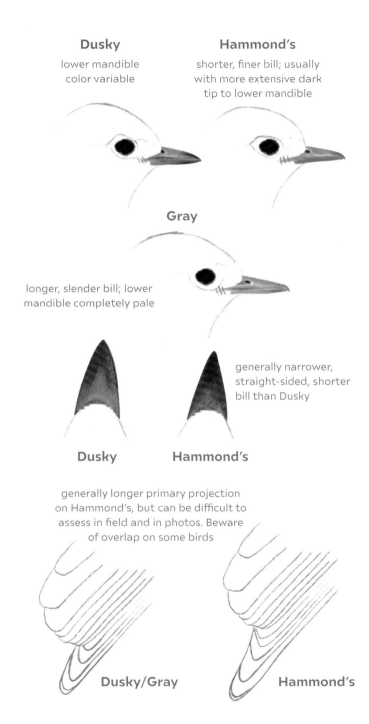

Dusky
lower mandible color variable

Hammond's
shorter, finer bill; usually with more extensive dark tip to lower mandible

Gray

longer, slender bill; lower mandible completely pale

Dusky

Hammond's
generally narrower, straight-sided, shorter bill than Dusky

generally longer primary projection on Hammond's, but can be difficult to assess in field and in photos. Beware of overlap on some birds

Dusky/Gray

Hammond's

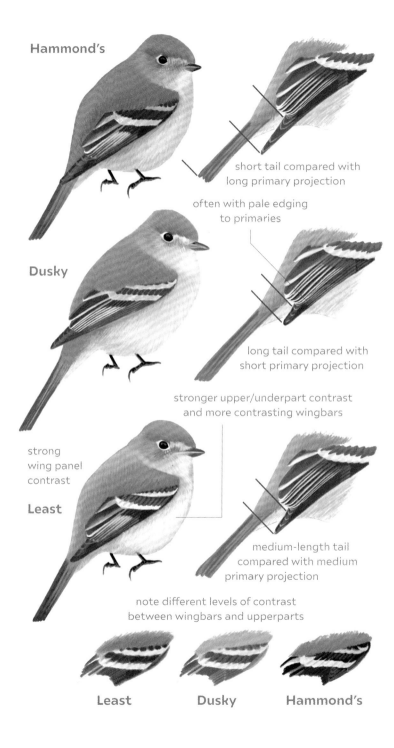

Hammond's

short tail compared with
long primary projection

often with pale edging
to primaries

Dusky

long tail compared with
short primary projection

stronger upper/underpart contrast
and more contrasting wingbars

strong
wing panel
contrast

Least

medium-length tail
compared with medium
primary projection

note different levels of contrast
between wingbars and upperparts

Least   Dusky   Hammond's

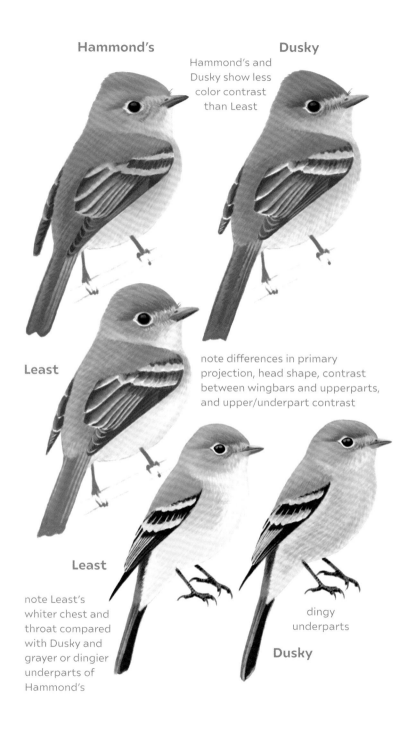

Hammond's

Dusky

Hammond's and Dusky show less color contrast than Least

Least

note differences in primary projection, head shape, contrast between wingbars and upperparts, and upper/underpart contrast

Least

note Least's whiter chest and throat compared with Dusky and grayer or dingier underparts of Hammond's

dingy underparts

Dusky

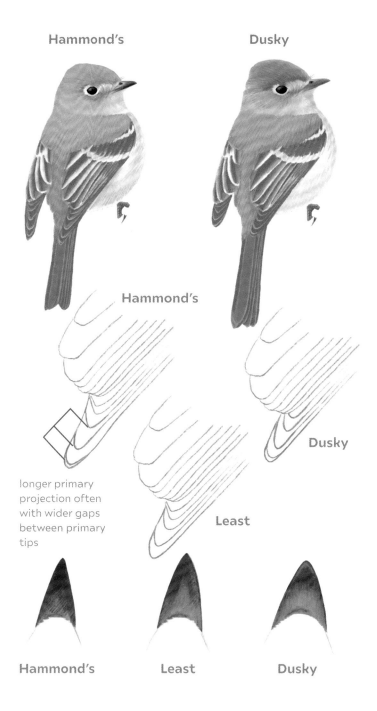

Hammond's

Dusky

Hammond's

Dusky

Least

longer primary
projection often
with wider gaps
between primary
tips

Hammond's

Least

Dusky

Hammond's

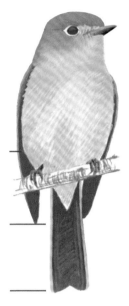

short tail relative to
long wings; small,
thin, dark bill

Dusky

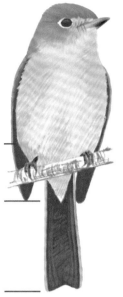

long tail relative to
short wings; medium-
width, dusky-tipped bill

Least

medium-length tail
relative to medium
wings; wider bill

Pacific-slope

relatively
long tail

EMPIDONAX CALL NOTE COMPARISON

Least, Dusky, Gray and Willow all give *"whit"* calls while Hammond's gives a *"pip"* call. Dusky's call is more inflected, giving it a more liquid quality. Least's spectrogram is shorter, steeper, lower frequency and has a strong harmonic, giving it a sharper, more husky quality than Dusky. Gray's *"whit"* is shorter and higher pitched than Least and Dusky. Willow's call is longer and starts from a lower frequency, giving it the most liquid quality of these *Empidonax*.

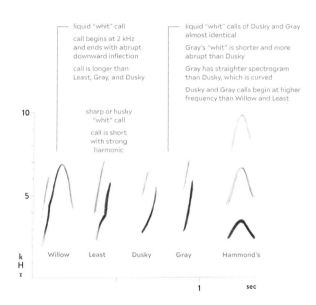

liquid "whit" call

call begins at 2 kHz and ends with abrupt downward inflection

call is longer than Least, Gray, and Dusky

liquid "whit" calls of Dusky and Gray almost identical

Gray's "whit" is shorter and more abrupt than Dusky

Gray has straighter spectrogram than Dusky, which is curved

Dusky and Gray calls begin at higher frequency than Willow and Least

sharp or husky "whit" call

call is short with strong harmonic

10

5

Willow   Least   Dusky   Gray   Hammond's

k
H
z

1   sec

Pine Flycatcher
Empidonax affinis
L 5.1–5.7" (13.0–14.5 cm), WT 0.4 oz (11.5 g)

GENERAL IDENTIFICATION Pine Flycatcher is phylogenetically a sister species to Dusky. It typically has an overall gray plumage (like Gray), but it otherwise has a remarkable resemblance to a dull Pacific-slope or Cordilleran with its medium-sized bill, all orange lower mandible, peaked or slightly crested crown, medium to long primary projection, relatively long tail, slender build, distinct eye-ring with elongated rear (teardrop-like), relatively bold wingbars, and a weak wing panel contrast due to strong pale edges to primary and secondary feathers. Voice is probably the most reliable way to identify Pine. However, there are subtle structural differences that may help in distinguishing it from Pacific-slope and Cordilleran. In addition to the overall duller coloration, Pine's tail is often distinctly forked, unlike Pacific-slope and Cordilleran and most other *Empidonax*. Pine also has a steep forehead angle, approaching that of Hammond's, whereas Pacific-slope and Cordilleran have a shallower forehead angle. Pine's steep forehead angle also quickly transitions to a shallower slope, resulting in a "kinked" or "angled" forehead profile. In Pacific-slope and Cordilleran, the slope of the forehead from the bill to the crown is smoother. Pine may occasionally show pale outer-tail feathers like Gray, a feature not seen in Pacific-slope and Cordilleran.

VOICE Pine has a distinctive song, "*pip puweee*" or "*pip pip pewee*," with the last note drawn out and sometimes burry. Its calls include a sharp "*pip*" and "*whit*," the former like Dusky and the latter like Willow, Gray, Dusky, and Least. Pine also gives a high-pitch, thin "*tseet*" call reminiscent of a titmouse, nearly identical to Pacific-slope and Cordilleran "*tseet*" calls.

PINE FLYCATCHER

relatively weak wing panel contrast

long primary projection

typically dull or gray in overall color but bright individuals very similar to Cordilleran

long tail, often with fork

Pine

Dusky

Cordilleran

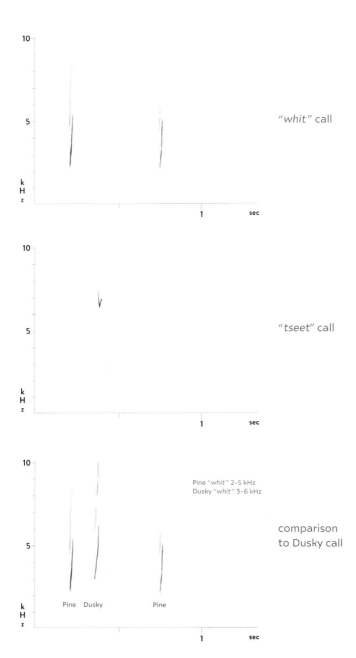

"*whit*" call

"*tseet*" call

Pine "*whit*" 2–5 kHz
Dusky "*whit*" 3–6 kHz

comparison
to Dusky call

Pine Dusky   Pine

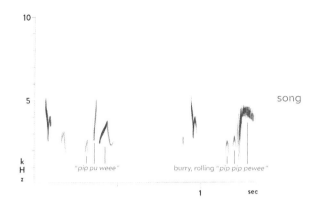

song

"pip pu weee"   burry, rolling "pip pip pewee"

PINE FLYCATCHER

RANGE AND HABITAT Pine Flycatcher is a resident of arid, open pine and oak forests in the mountains of Mexico and Central America. As of June 2022, there have been only two records north of Mexico, both in the mountains of southeast Arizona: a summering bird in the Santa Rita mountains from 28 May–7 July, 2016 and another in the Catalina Mountains in late May, 2022. Given its remarkable similarity to Cordilleran, this bird may often be overlooked. Late spring/early summer may be the best time to search for wandering Pines in the mountains of Arizona and possibly west Texas.

SIMILAR SPECIES Pine is very similar in structure to Pacific-slope and Cordilleran (see above discussion), but note Pine's duller coloration and longer, frequently forked tail, as well as differences in head shape. Gray, Hammond's, and Dusky Flycatchers may also pose identification problems. Gray and Pine have similar coloration, but Gray has a shorter primary projection, longer tail, and the distinctive behavior of dropping its tail like a phoebe. Pine has a shorter tail and longer primary projection than Dusky. Gray and Dusky also do not have forked tails. Hammond's has a much smaller bill, generally all dark lower mandible, stronger wing panel contrast, and shorter tail.

Gray Flycatcher

Empidonax wrightii

L 5.5–5.7″ (14.0–14.5 cm), WT 0.40–0.51 oz (11.3–14.5 g)

GENERAL IDENTIFICATION Gray Flycatcher is one of the more distinctive *Empidonax*. It is the palest, longest tailed, and longest billed of all *Empidonax*. Its short to medium primary projection accentuates its long-tailed look. It has a flattish crown and shallow forehead angle. It has the weakest wing panel and wingbar contrast of all *Empidonax*. Its lower mandible is almost always entirely orange. An eye-ring is always present but may not always stand out against its pale gray face. Its chest is pale gray and similar to its upperparts, resulting in weak upper/underpart contrast. Outer-tail feathers are whitish, and when seen well, this feature is generally diagnostic. Gray occasionally flicks its wings, but the most distinctive behavior is its habitual tail dropping, reminiscent of Eastern Phoebe (*Sayornis phoebe*), in which the tail is rapidly brought upward but then dropped back downward more slowly. Adult undergoes complete prebasic molt on wintering grounds.

On both nesting and wintering grounds, Gray prefers dry, open habitats with scattered shrubs and is particularly fond of sagebrush habitats. It is unlikely to be found in wooded habitats except during migration, but even then it will typically be found in open shrubby areas or in woodland edges. Gray usually forages only a few feet above the ground, almost never in the canopy of tall trees.

VOICE Most common call is a short rising "*whit*" like Dusky, Least, and Willow. Call is less emphatic/energetic than Least and slightly shorter than Dusky and Willow. Dawn song consists of a two-note "*che-bec*" somewhat like Least, often given in pairs, and accompanied occasionally by brief twitters. Single note whistled "*peeo*" call is like that of Hammond's and Dusky but more descending than Dusky and less quickly descending than Hammond's.

GRAY FLYCATCHER

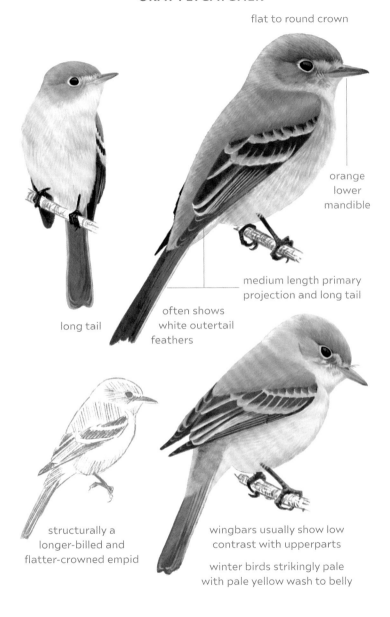

flat to round crown

orange
lower
mandible

medium length primary
projection and long tail

long tail

often shows
white outertail
feathers

structurally a
longer-billed and
flatter-crowned empid

wingbars usually show low
contrast with upperparts

winter birds strikingly pale
with pale yellow wash to belly

GRAY FLYCATCHER

long, straight bill, long tail, and round to flat head gives distinctive structural look

dull wing bars

in good light, pale gray birds can show pale olive/green wash to upperparts

dips tail downward in deliberate fashion

low upper/underpart contrast

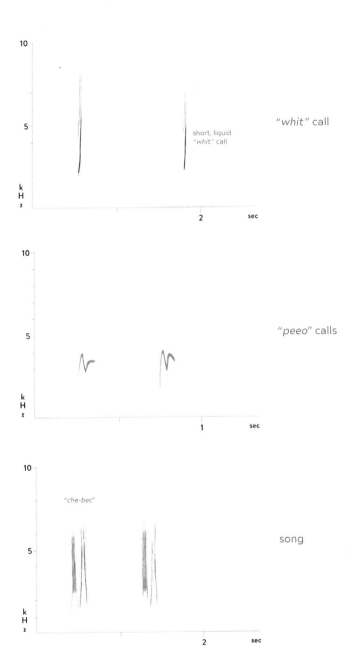

"*whit*" call

short, liquid
"*whit*" call

"*peeo*" calls

"*che-bec*"

song

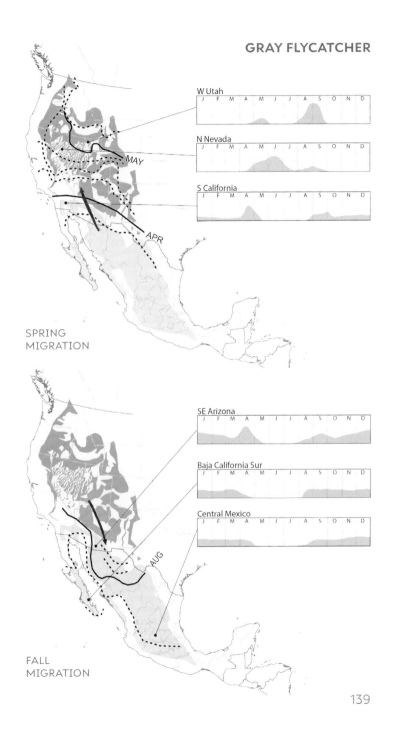

GRAY FLYCATCHER

W Utah
J F M A M J J A S O N D

N Nevada
J F M A M J J A S O N D

S California
J F M A M J J A S O N D

MAY

APR

SPRING
MIGRATION

SE Arizona
J F M A M J J A S O N D

Baja California Sur
J F M A M J J A S O N D

Central Mexico
J F M A M J J A S O N D

AUG

FALL
MIGRATION

RANGE AND HABITAT Gray Flycatcher breeds in open brushlands and woodlands in the arid American west. It can be found in open sagebrush, pinyon/juniper forests and ponderosa pine habitats. It winters in the southwestern United States and Mexico. Gray is a relatively short-distance migrant. Spring migrants begin passing through southern California and Arizona by early Mar., peaking in mid-Apr., and continue through the first week of May. It arrives on breeding grounds by mid-Apr. and departs from breeding grounds in early July. Fall migrants begin passing through the southwestern United States in late July and early Aug., with passage complete by early Oct. Migrating Grays tend to avoid the immediate coast, preferring to migrate through the more arid deserts or valleys of the continental interior. It is a very rare stray to eastern United States in fall and winter.

SIMILAR SPECIES Gray is less often confused with other flycatchers due to its overall pale coloration, long tail, long bill, and elongate body, but confusion can still occur with Dusky and Hammond's. Gray has a longer bill, a longer tail, weaker wing panel and wingbar contrast, and more extensive orange lower mandible. Hammond's is darker with long primary projection, short tail, small bill, and steep forehead. Willow, particularly in the west, is superficially like Gray, but note Willow's shorter and wider tail. Willow does not flick or pump its tail. Note that Gray frequents open habitats with scattered shrubs and is unlikely to be found in forests or foraging within the canopy of tall trees.

Least Flycatcher

Empidonax minimus

L 4.9–5.5″ (12.5–14.0 cm), WT 0.28–0.46 oz (8–13 g)

GENERAL IDENTIFICATION Least Flycatcher is the most common flycatcher in the east and the most likely eastern flycatcher vagrant in the west, so becoming familiar with Least is recommended. Least is a small, compact, big-headed, and short-tailed *Empidonax*. Primary projection is distinctly short (projection may appear artificially longer if the secondaries stack is spread out). Bright wingbars and dark ground color of wing result in strong wingbar contrast. Wingbars also contrast with upperparts. General lack of pale edges to primary feathers results in strong wing panel contrast. White chest and underparts contrast with upperparts. Crown is round with moderate forehead angle. Lower mandible is completely pale. Bill is small with broad base. Tail is narrow, often narrowing slightly toward body. Eye-ring is full and bold, but often diffuse and sometimes thinner at the top. Lores are often pale. Least habitually flicks wings and tail. It typically forages at low to mid-canopy and on the outer edges of shrubs and trees. Prebasic molt begins on summering grounds, but it is completed (flight feathers) on wintering grounds.

VOICE Least emits an abrupt rising "*whit*" like Dusky, Willow, and Gray, but it is shorter, sharper, and more abrupt. Least's "*whit*" spectrogram is straighter and less inflected than Dusky. Least's "*whit*" also has a strong harmonic, giving it a more energetic call than Dusky, Willow, and Gray (see comparison spectrograms on page 129). Often likened to the sharp, husky call of Yellow-rumped "Audubon's" Warbler. Song, mostly given at dawn, is a hard "*che-bek*," often given in rapid continuous succession.

LEAST FLYCATCHER

strong upper/underpart contrast

strong wing panel contrast

short primary projection

short, narrow tail

rounded crown

messy eye-ring

bold wingbars

whitish underparts

10

strong
upper
harmonic

5

k
H
z

1   sec

sharp *"whit"* call
with harmonic

10

5

k
H
z

1   sec

"che-bek" song

RANGE AND HABITAT Least is the most common *Empidonax* of the northern forests, ranging from western Canada east to Quebec and south across the northern United States. Breeding range extends south along the Appalachians. Least can be found from semi-open woodlands to forest edges and shrubby areas, preferring understory and inner canopy. It winters in Mexico and Central America with small numbers wintering along coasts of Texas and southern Florida. Spring migrants take a western circum-Gulf path through Texas and then move north through the mid-continent after reaching east Texas. Fall migrants mostly return on the same circum-Gulf path but an eastward shift in migration path leads to large numbers passing through Louisiana on their way to Texas or to local wintering grounds in Florida. Least arrives in mid-Apr. along the Texas coast, earlier than Yellow-bellied, Willow, and Alder. Spring migrants continue into mid- to late May with arrival on breeding grounds in May. Fall migrants pass through between early Aug. and early Oct., with the first wintering birds appearing in Mexico in mid-Aug. It is a rare but regular vagrant to the Pacific coast in late fall (late spring vagrancy to the Pacific coast is also possible, but numbers are reduced compared with fall).

SIMILAR SPECIES Least Flycatcher is often misidentified as another species of flycatcher if one is not familiar with this species. Acadian is similar because it has a white throat, strong upper/underpart contrast, and relatively bold wingbars, but note Acadian's wide and straight-margined tail, much longer primary projection (and elongated outer primary spacing compared with more uniform primary spacing in Least), shallow forehead angle, and cleaner, crisper full eye-ring. Yellow-bellied, especially dull individuals, is easily confused with a bright Least, but focus on Yellow-bellied's weaker upper/underpart contrast, longer primary projection, and crisper and more uniform eye-ring. Surprisingly, Least is often misidentified as Alder, but seldom is Alder misidentified as Least

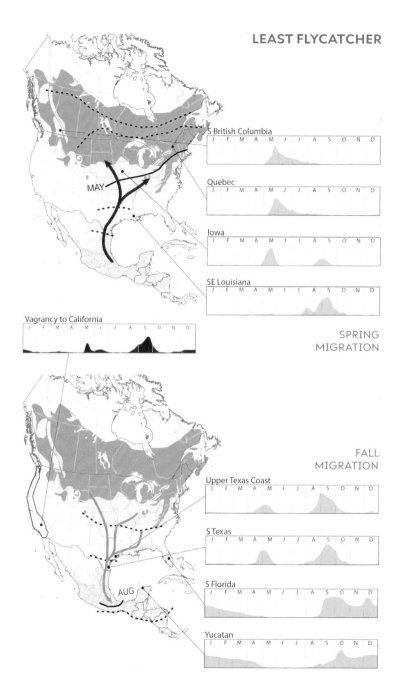

LEAST FLYCATCHER

S British Columbia

Quebec

Iowa

SE Louisiana

Vagrancy to California

SPRING
MIGRATION

MAY

FALL
MIGRATION

Upper Texas Coast

S Texas

S Florida

Yucatan

AUG

145

(see comparison plate on page 87). Note Alder's wider tail, thinner and sometimes nonexistent eye-ring, longer primary projection, and duller wingbar contrast. In the west, Hammond's and Dusky can cause confusion (see comparisons on pages 125–28). Hammond's has much longer primary projection, weak upper/underpart contrast, and steep forehead angle. Dusky tends to be duller with longer tail, and weaker wingbar and wing panel contrast. Beware when Least holds its secondaries in a spread-out manner. This can give the impression of long primary projection, often the source of erroneous Hammond's or Dusky Flycatcher identifications in the east.

Buff-breasted Flycatcher
Empidonax fulvifrons
L 5.1″ (13 cm), WT 0.28 oz (8 g)

GENERAL IDENTIFICATION The Buff-breasted Flycatcher is the smallest and brightest-colored *Empidonax*, aptly named because of its distinct cinnamon wash across its breast, a feature that is not shared by any other regularly occurring flycatcher in the United States. Other field marks, however, should be noted, especially for birds in worn plumage, which may have lost their cinnamon tones. Buff-breasted has a distinct but somewhat fuzzy eye-ring, a proportionately large head, round crown, short- to medium-length bill, medium-length primary projection, and medium to long tail. Its lower mandible is completely orange. Its wing pattern is also distinctive, with relatively bold wingbars that are often whitish and contrast with the overall buffy plumage. The wing ground color is relatively dark, which also accentuates the wingbar contrast. It has very pale edges to secondaries and medium-pale edges to primaries, giving it a moderate wing panel contrast. Buff-breasted occasionally flicks its wings and tail. It tends to perch in the mid-canopy.

VOICE Buff-breasted emits a short, but hard "*pit*" call, more akin to an Indigo Bunting than to the more whistled or hollow "*whit*" calls of other *Empidonax*. Its song consists of a series of squeaky two-note phrases, "*pirrip pirrip pu-reee*," interspersed with brief twitters.

RANGE AND HABITAT Buff-breasted Flycatcher is primarily found in open pine-oak forests of the mountains of Mexico and Central America. Its range expands in spring and summer to the mountains of southeastern Arizona and the Davis Mountains of west Texas, arriving in mid-Mar. and continuing through mid-Sept. In Mexico, Buff-breasted moves from its breeding range down to lower elevations in winter. It is otherwise not known to wander far from its

BUFF-BREASTED FLYCATCHER

bright, colorful
"cute" empid

bright orangish
or buff underparts

paler birds with more olive
upperparts and paler underparts
may have superficial resemblance
to Cordilleran

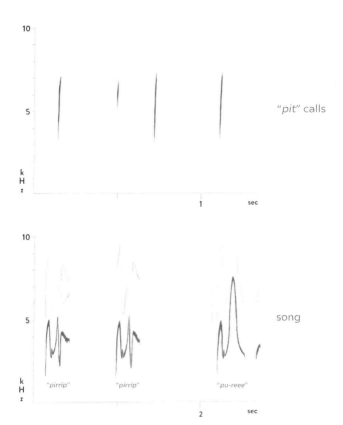

"*pit*" calls

song

"*pirrip*"   "*pirrip*"   "*pu-reee*"

normal range. There are two remarkable records of spring vagrants: one in each of southern California (Kern County, 15 May, 2016) and Colorado (El Paso County, 19 May, 1991).

SIMILAR SPECIES Typically, the cinnamon coloration to the breast is enough to eliminate all other flycatchers except for Tufted, but Tufted has a pointed crest. Slightly worn birds or birds not seen in good light can be confused with other flycatchers with similar structures, such as Hammond's, Least, and perhaps Pacific-slope/Cordilleran. Hammond's has a darker and duskier chest, and longer primary projection. Hammond's will never show a completely orange lower mandible. Least can generally be ruled out by range, but it has a white and contrasting chest. In addition, Least has a strong wing panel contrast. Pacific-slope's and Cordilleran's crest and yellow-green coloration makes it unlikely to be confused with Buff-breasted. Buff-breasted has a rounded crown and never shows greenish tones.

BUFF-BREASTED FLYCATCHER

SE Arizona

J F M A M J J A S O N D

Bibliography

Allen, M. C., Napoli, M. M., Sheehan, J., Master, T. L., Pyle, P., Whitehead, D. R., and Taylor, T., 2020, Acadian Flycatcher (*Empidonax virescens*), version 1.0. Birds of the World (P. G. Rodewald, Editor). Cornell Lab of Ornithology, Ithaca, NY, USA. https://doi.org/10.2173/bow.acafly.01

Altman, B. and Sallabanks, R., 2020, Olive-sided Flycatcher (*Contopus cooperi*), version 1.0. Birds of the World (A. F. Poole, Editor). Cornell Lab of Ornithology, Ithaca, NY, USA. https://doi.org/10.2173/bow.olsfly.01

Bemis, C. and Rising, J. D., 2020, Western Wood-Pewee (*Contopus sordidulus*), version 1.0. Birds of the World (A. F. Poole and F. B. Gill, Editors). Cornell Lab of Ornithology, Ithaca, NY, USA. https://doi.org/10.2173/bow.wewpew.01

Bowers Jr., R. K. and Dunning, J. B., Jr., 2020, Buff-breasted Flycatcher (*Empidonax fulvifrons*), version 1.0. Birds of the World (A. F. Poole and F. B. Gill, Editors). Cornell Lab of Ornithology, Ithaca, NY, USA. https://doi.org/10.2173/bow.bubfly.01

Chace, J. F. and Tweit, R. C., 2020, Greater Pewee (*Contopus pertinax*), version 1.0. Birds of the World (A. F. Poole and F. B. Gill, Editors). Cornell Lab of Ornithology, Ithaca, NY, USA. https://doi.org/10.2173/bow.grepew.01

Dunning, J. B., Jr., 1984, *Body Weights of 686 Species of North American Birds.* Western Bird Banding Association Monograph, no. 1. *Eldon Publishing*, Cave Creek, AZ, USA.

Farnsworth, A. and Lebbin, D. J., 2020, Pine Flycatcher (*Empidonax affinis*), version 1.0. Birds of the World (J. del Hoyo, A. Elliott, J. Sargatal, D. A. Christie, and E. de Juana, Editors). Cornell Lab of Ornithology, Ithaca, NY, USA. https://doi.org/10.2173/bow.pinfly1.01

Farnsworth, A. and Lebbin, D. J., 2020, Cuban Pewee (*Contopus caribaeus*), version 1.0. Birds of the World (J. del Hoyo, A. Elliott, J. Sargatal, D. A. Christie, and E. de Juana, Editors). Cornell Lab of Ornithology, Ithaca, NY, USA. https://doi.org/10.2173/bow.cubpew1.01

Farnsworth, A. and Lebbin, D. J. 2020, Tufted Flycatcher (*Mitrephanes phaeocercus*), version 1.0. Birds of the World (J. del Hoyo, A. Elliott, J. Sargatal, D. A. Christie, and E. de Juana, Editors). Cornell Lab of Ornithology, Ithaca, NY, USA. https://doi.org/10.2173/bow.tuffly.01

Fjeldså, J., Ohlson, J. I., Batalha-Filho, H., Ericson, P. G. P., and Irestedt, M., 2018, Rapid expansion and diversification into new niche space by fluvicoline flycatchers. *Avian Biology* e01661, doi:10.1111/jav.01661.

Gross, D. A. and Lowther, P. E., 2020, Yellow-bellied Flycatcher (*Empidonax flaviventris*), version 1.0. Birds of the World (A. F. Poole, Editor). Cornell Lab of Ornithology, Ithaca, NY, USA. https://doi.org/10.2173/bow.yebfly.01

Harvey, M. G., Bravo, G. A., Claramunt, S., Cuervo, A. M., Derryberry, G. E., Battilana, J., Seeholzer, G. F., McKay, J. S., O'Meara, B. C., Faircloth, B. C., and Edwards, S. V., 2020, The evolution of a tropical biodiversity hotspot. *Science* 370:1343–1348.

Johnson, N. K. and Cicero, C., 2002, The role of ecological diversification in sibling speciation of *Empidonax* flycatchers (Tyrannidae): multigene evidence from mtDNA. *Molecular Ecology* 11: 2065–2081.

Kaufman, K., 1990, *A Field Guide to Advanced Birding: Birding Challenges and How to Approach Them. Houghton Mifflin*, Boston, MA, USA.

Lee, C. T., Birch, A., and Eubanks, T. L., 2008, Field identification of Western and Eastern wood-pewees. *Birding*, 40(4): 34–40.

Lowther, P. E., 2020, Alder Flycatcher (*Empidonax alnorum*), version 1.0. Birds of the World (A. F. Poole and F. B. Gill, Editors). Cornell Lab of Ornithology, Ithaca, NY, USA. https://doi.org/10.2173/bow.aldfly.01

McCallum, A., 2005, A comparison of major sounds of the Western Flycatcher complex, http://www.appliedbioacoustics.com/Repertoires/Passeriformes/ Tyrannidae/Empidonaxdifficilis/

McCallum, A., 2008, A comparison of the vocal repertoires of Willow Flycatcher *Empidonax traillii*) and Alder Flycatcher (*Empidonax alnorum*), http:// www.appliedbioacoustics.com/Repertoires/Passeriformes/Tyrannidae/ Empidonaxalnorum/bird.html

McCallum, A. 2011, Western Empids, http://www.appliedbioacoustics.com/ fieldguide/EmpFrame.html

McCallum, A., 2020, The Five Eastern North American Species of Genus *Empidonax*? http://www.archmccallum.com/Ear/Projects/fgu/ EmpEastIndex.html

Pereyra, M. E. and Sedgwick, J. A., 2020, Dusky Flycatcher (*Empidonax oberholseri*), version 1.0. Birds of the World (A. F. Poole, Editor). Cornell Lab of Ornithology, Ithaca, NY, USA. https://doi.org/10.2173/bow.dusfly.01

Phillips, A. R., Howe, M. A., and Lanyon, W. E., 1966, Identification of the flycatchers of eastern North America, with special emphasis on the genus *Empidonax. Bird-Banding*, 37(3): 153–171.

Phillips, A. R. and Lanyon, W. E., 1970, Additional notes on the flycatchers of eastern North America. *Bird-Banding*, 41(3): 190–197.

Pieplow, N., 2017, *Peterson Field Guide to Bird Sounds of Eastern North America*. Peterson Field Guides. *Mariner Books*, Boston, MA, USA.

Pieplow, N., 2019, *Peterson Field Guide to Bird Sounds of Western North America*. Peterson Field Guides, *Houghton Mifflin Harcourt*, Boston, MA, USA.

Pyle, P., 1997, *Identification Guide to North American Birds*, part I. *Slate Creek Press*, Bolinas, CA, USA.

Sedgwick, J. A., 2020, Hammond's Flycatcher (*Empidonax hammondii*), version 1.0. Birds of the World (A. F. Poole and F. B. Gill, Editors). Cornell Lab of Ornithology, Ithaca, NY, USA. https://doi.org/10.2173/bow.hamfly.01

Sedgwick, J. A., 2020, Willow Flycatcher (*Empidonax traillii*), version 1.0. Birds of the World (A. F. Poole and F. B. Gill, Editors). Cornell Lab of Ornithology, Ithaca, NY, USA. https://doi.org/10.2173/bow.wilfly.01

Sibley, D., 2014, *The Sibley Guide to Birds*, 2nd ed. Knopf, New York, NY, USA.

Tarof, S. and Briskie, J. V., 2020, Least Flycatcher (*Empidonax minimus*), version 1.0. Birds of the World (A. F. Poole, Editor). Cornell Lab of Ornithology, Ithaca, NY, USA. https://doi.org/10.2173/bow.leafly.01

Watt, D. J., McCarty, J. P., Kendrick, S. W., Newell, F. L., and Pyle, P., 2020, Eastern Wood-Pewee (*Contopus virens*), version 1.0. Birds of the World (P. G. Rodewald, Editor). Cornell Lab of Ornithology, Ithaca, NY, USA. https://doi.org/10.2173/bow.eawpew.01

Whitney, B. and Kaufman, K., 1985, The *Empidonax* challenge. Part I: Introduction. *Birding* 17:151–158.

Whitney, B. and Kaufman, K., 1985, The *Empidonax* challenge. Part II: Least, Hammond's, and Dusky Flycatchers. *Birding* 17:277–287.

Whitney, B. and Kaufman, K., 1986, The *Empidonax* challenge. Part III: Willow and Alder Flycatchers: *Birding* 18:153–159.

Whitney, B. and Kaufman, K., 1986, The *Empidonax* challenge. Part IV: Acadian, Yellow-bellied, and Western Flycatchers. *Birding* 18:315–327.

Whitney, B. and Kaufman, K., 1987, The *Empidonax* challenge. Part V: Gray and Buff-breasted Flycatchers. *Birding* 19:7–15.

Useful Websites

Cornell Laboratory of Ornithology eBird–collection of bird images, sounds, and geospatial and temporal data on bird status (https://ebird.org)

Macaulay Library for bird information and resources including bird sounds (www.macaulaylibrary.org)

xeno-canto.org—a collection of bird sounds from around the world (https://xeno-canto.org)

Peterson Field Guide to Bird Sounds by Nathan Pieplow (https://academy.allaboutbirds.org/peterson-field-guide-to-bird-sounds)

Index